This brave, occasionally moving and often hilarious memoir traces Muggins's relationships with Japanese women over the course of two decades. Few books set in contemporary Asian societies have been as successful at pulling the reader into the cultural milieu and making the foreign familiar.

The author protests perhaps too strongly that *How to Pick Up Japanese Chicks...* should not be mistaken for a self-help manual. In fact the smiles, the belly-laughs, the wistful *there but for the grace of God go I* nods that every page elicits testify that it is the best sort of therapy for anyone suffering from relationship fatigue anywhere, anytime.

Josh Muggins published several noted magazine pieces on life in Japan in the late 1980s and early 1990s before slithering down a dank and putrid hole into which, at the behest of Japanese women everywhere, he will promptly return upon the publication of this book. He welcomes comments at the address below.

joshmuggins@hotmail.com

*Learn the author's time-tested secrets
in 12 easy lessons!*

**Worldly disgrace <u>and</u>
eternal damnation guaranteed!**

How To Pick Up Japanese Chicks

And Doom Your Immortal Soul

by

Josh Muggins

*1663 LIBERTY DRIVE, SUITE 200
BLOOMINGTON, INDIANA 47403
(800) 839-8640
<u>WWW.AUTHORHOUSE.COM</u>*

© 2005 Josh Muggins. All Rights Reserved.

No part of this book may be reproduced, stored in a retrieval system, or transmitted by any means, electronic, mechanical, photocopying, recording, or otherwise, without written permission from the author.

First published by AuthorHouse 03/05/05

ISBN: 1-4208-2046-X (e)
ISBN: 1-4208-2045-1 (sc)

Printed in the United States of America
Bloomington, Indiana

This book is printed on acid-free paper.

Cover design by Gary Pettis

Disclaimers and Crap

Disclaimer 1

As the last five words of the title make plain, this is *not* a self-help book. Any person purchasing this book in the belief that it will in any way improve his sexual opportunities with any form of female—Japanese, American, Eurasian, lobotomized, Romulan, ovine, superannuated, somnambulant, or any combination of the above—relinquishes all claims to refunds or litigation. He does, however, retain his God-given right to whine about his blunder, with the caveat that so doing invites the clandestine ridicule of coworkers there at the fast-food franchise.

Disclaimer 2

This book is a work of fiction. I know this because a friend who test-read for me told me so. "This is a great novel, and I really like the way you've woven incidents and people from your own life into it," he began. "But it *is* a novel, *right?*"

He then went on to enumerate several unpleasant consequences that would befall me at our next face-to-face encounter if everything in this book, especially the final three chapters, were true. So fiction it is.

Even if this were a bona fide autobiography—here comes more weasel-wording; did I mention that Bill Clinton is my all-time favorite president?—it would be a mishmash of events and conversations reconstructed years or even decades after the fact, and thus of highly dubious accuracy.

This is not to say that I would massage those events and conversations to make myself look noble. Believe me, if that were the goal I could have done a much better job of it because I'm a good writer.

I'm *good*, I tell you! Maybe that comes off sounding more than a little like Fredo Corleone screeching "I'm *smart*! I'm *smart*!" to Michael just before setting out on his one-way fishing expedition at Lake Tahoe, and maybe I should dwell on that analogy a little more...but it's too late now.

Note:

It occurred to me on my final read-through that the concept for the "West Yokohama Diet" bit in Lesson 10 owes a heavy debt to a parody published in *National Lampoon* circa 1980. The borrowing was unintentional; apologies to the authors, whose names cannot be retrieved.

Contents

FOREWORD...x

LESSON 1
Get your sorry white ass to Japan 4

LESSON 2
Do not be furry 9

LESSON 3
Be used and discarded like a mindless tool,
and learn to love it 39

LESSON 4
Don't do anything 55

LESSON 5
The cistern of your lust 70

LESSON 6
Know when to fold 'em 85

LESSON 7
The fear of God..95

LESSON 8
First, do no harm 124

LESSON 9
Reality is not your friend..159

LESSON 10
Honor thy father and thy mother..189

LESSON 11
Or Stage Five—The Moment of Clarity................................220

LESSON 12
The cabinet of Dr. Katagiri...233

AFTERWORD
Time keeps on slippin' (slippin', slippin')
into the fewwww-cherrrrr 244

FOREWORD

There's this moment from the original *Star Trek* that resonates all the more with every passing year. I'm pretty sure it's the one where the intergalactic shoplifters filch Spock's brain.

Here's how I recall it, with no claims to accuracy:

Kirk and McCoy have beamed down to a cold, rocky planet and are set upon by a ragtag pack of shaggy Caucasoid males. Bringing firepower to bear and perhaps sloughing off yet another surplus landing party volunteer, our heroes quickly prevail and begin to interrogate a captive.

Kirk being Kirk, the chitchat soon enough shifts to women—but bogs down when both the word and the concept baffle the native. This does not come as a shock given his makeover-begging grooming habits but, as McCoy points out, none of them would have been born to enjoy this cheery encounter among the Styrofoam boulders had it not been for women.

When the concept of female personages finally does seep into the primitive's mind, he recoils with horror.

"Ah," he rasps, "the givers of pain…and delight!"

—◻—

Turns out that the whole zany world is run by an ancient computer ensconced deep under ground.

The computer—no fool, it—has surrounded itself with all the females on the planet, who attend to its upkeep dressed in sheer, flimsy, Kirk-teasing costumes.

To ensure a continuing workforce of such caretakers, the computer compels the women to venture up to the planet's surface from time to time, coldcock all the males with some sort of vicious, wide-scan coldcocking doohickey, drag their senseless carcasses down below, show them a good time, and then cast them back onto the planet's frigid hellscape—with an unaccountable spring in their step for the next day of hunter-gathering, presumably.

Russian orphanages, one would think, could save them a lot of muss and fuss.

—◻—

Here's the point:

I am a shaggy Caucasoid-American male who has lived in Japan for twenty-five years.

For any male readers who have had contact with Japanese female life forms during this quarter century, no further explanation is needed. The rest really ought to slog through this book.

For starters, think of the relationship between Japanese chicks and shaggy Caucasoid males as much like that of a boy and his dog—one of those timeless, effortless mutual affinities that overleaps all such obstacles as differing languages and excessive slobbering. And if you have to ask which one corresponds to the dog in this analogy, stop reading now. You're beyond help.

—◻—

This is probably as good a time as any to admit that this book is an absolute fraud. To anyone who has bought it on the assumption that it provides useful tips on connecting with Japanese women, I say: Sorry. The same goes for those who expected something, well, like, *good*; or anything but the self-indulgent memoir which, frankly, this is.

Even a self-indulgent memoirist has to eat, though; ergo the seductive title. As there remains the danger that some will skim through the book before purchasing, I have protracted the diabolical self-help-book ruse by organizing it as a series of "lessons." Book marketing, as Jules in *Pulp Fiction* might have put it, is some pretty cold-blooded shit.

—▫—

On the bright side, the spectacular ineptitude of my Japanese chick pick-upping may at the least serve to boost the male reader's ego.

Failure can be a powerful teacher. You may agree with Henry Ford that "failure is the opportunity to begin again more intelligently." If so, more power to you. You may also agree with Henry Ford that Nazism is a pretty darn good idea. But I hope not.

In any event, how much the better to learn from the failures of others than from your own! The architects of Pisa have racked up over eight centuries and counting of rigorously upright tower building. Could they have achieved this mark without the constant shadow of failure lurching over them?

Here, then, are one man's leaning towers: twelve lessons in the utter futility of dealing with Japanese chicks. Most recount failures; a few describe successes.

The failures I look back upon fondly and describe without the slightest twinge of pain. It was the successes—one in particular—that almost did me in.

LESSON 1

Get your sorry white ass to Japan

You can find Japanese chicks almost anywhere in the world. They resemble cosmic dust motes and lecherous clergymen in this way, and only in this way. Millions are abroad at any given moment, working, studying, shopping or just browsing.

This is partly my doing. Here in Japan it is my job, nay my privilege, to prepare Japanese chicks to study abroad in English-medium colleges throughout the world.

It has its benefits; I'm often the recipient of savage, full-frontal hugs when our university posts the study-abroad scholarship list.[*]

Anyway, thanks to me, you can now encounter Japanese chicks in the environs of universities from Los Angeles to New York to London to Sydney to Mombassa to Toronto to Cardiff to Johannesburg to Manila to Tuscaloosa. I hear that new-fangled drafting school over to Crabwell Corners has five of them in residence this term.

Alas, this Diaspora of Japanese Chick Nation does not work to the advantage of the average shaggy Caucasoid-American male. If we examine the reasons why such a great many Japanese chicks have chosen to leave their homeland to

---

[*] I got one just the other day, in fact, and it saddened me. The ensuing palpitations and rubbery legs served as reminders that savage, full-frontal hugs now define the upper limit of Japanese-chick-induced stimulation that my achy-breaky cardiovascular system can withstand.

study abroad, we find, to our slack-jawed astonishment, that they have done so mainly to *study*. Abroad.

In other words, they are not abroad in pursuit of shaggy Caucasoid-American companionship.* And even if they were, they would have a wide range of options that include many candidates who feel no need to buy a book called *How to Pick Up Japanese Chicks*.

—◻—

The studies are conclusive and unanimous:

The highest concentration of Japanese chicks in the world is to be found…in Japan.

As we all learned in junior high social studies, Japan is a nation of islands—the biggies being Honshu, Hokkaido, Kyushu, and that other one shaped like a fraying bowtie—along with thousands of smaller ones. Every one of these islands is chock-a-block with chicks. Thus, getting one's sorry white ass over to any of these islands would seem like a really good first step.

If the reader is dismayed to know that several thousand of us shaggy Caucasoid males have beaten you to the punch sorry-white-ass-emigration-wise, take comfort in knowing that many of us are over the hill or simply too drained from ceaseless sexual success to carry on.

Others, God help them, have become monogamous.[†]

---

[*] But don't try telling this to Japanese dudes. Not long ago four despondent sophomore lads dropped by to drown the sorrow of their chickless existences in drink, incontrovertibly convinced that it was their minuscule penises that were driving potential mates away.

"Have any chicks actually *seen* your penises?" I asked.

"No," they readily confessed. "But they *know*. Somehow, they *just know*."

[†] *Awkward transition alert*. Brace for a shockingly amateurish shift in tone. At this point, the book abandons all pretense of addressing the reader's needs and becomes all about me, me, me.

This really is the best I can write. Honest.

HOW TO PICK UP JAPANESE CHICKS

—◻—

As for *me*, I did the sorry-white-ass-emigration thing back in nineteen seventy-nine.

During my senior year at university—well, to be precise, my third senior year; when I find something I like, I stick with it—I sought work overseas and was granted a contract by an "English conversation" school in Tokyo.

Most job-seekers might have qualms about accepting a contract from some outfit half a world away that chose its employees on the basis of a cover letter and very short résumé, without so much as a telephone interview. But most job-seekers have not spent three years being a senior.

My first encounter with Japanese chicks occurred at the Narita Airport information desk. There were three of them on duty. They were primly uniformed. They were impeccably groomed. They were slim. And they were much aggrieved.

Aggrieved they were, because my predecessor in line was enraged at their inability to answer his questions. Uncannily channeling Coach Bob Knight in full technical foul mode, he leaned in close and sputtered at them.

The chicks remained cooler than any Big Ten officiating crew and tried to respond whenever their accuser paused to mop excess spittle off his chin. But he stalked off, unsatisfied, leaving three aggrieved faces behind.

I stepped forth and rolled my eyes in the universal sign for *What an asshole!*, which erased the grief from the chicks' faces and even caused them, in unison, to bring their hands to their mouths to mute a merry triad titter.

"Where…is…the…limousine….bus?" I asked, having learned through observation that rapid speech paved the road to grief. This brought even more hand-muted titters.

I was on a roll! At last, a country where my stuff works! Even when I'm not quite using it!

They directed me to the counter where I might buy a ticket and showed me the door through which I would exit to board the bus.

"This door right here?" I asked.

More titters still.

Is this a great country? Or what? (Answer: Both.)

I thanked them and boarded the bus that would take me toward my new home and away from them forever. But Ambition had sunk its talons into me.

I was doomed.

With a quarter century of hindsight and the wisdom of age, I can confidently reconstruct the discussion that ensued among them after I had passed from sight:

Chick 1: What a nice shaggy Caucasoid-American male!
Chick 2: Indeed! And did you not sense its size? Like a coiled cobra!
Chick 3: Aye! What a fine addition it would make to our brew!
Chick 1: Eye of newt and toe of toad…
All: Double, double, toil and trouble…

Teaching Point 1: To charm Japanese chicks, it is helpful not to be an asshole.

And so much the better if there is a bona fide asshole handy to whom you can contrast yourself. A desperate last resort would be to hire a "ringer asshole" to walk around with you, preceding you in lines at airports, cafeterias, bank counters and so on. (High-priced bars and health clubs in central Tokyo that cater to the expat business community could be good recruiting zones, and you know, I wish I'd thought of this sooner…)

This tactic will ensure at least a foot in the door toward success with Japanese chicks, as well as the eventual corrosion of your immortal soul.

LESSON 2

Do not be furry

O, wonder!
How many goodly creatures are there here!
How beauteous mankind is! O brave new world,
That has such people in't!

—The Tempest

I fucked that Tokiko chick last night.
Hopped all over the room with her.
It was great.

—Fat Matt, IHE senior instructor

The carpet layers, having labored all morning in the close, narrow corridors of the International House of English with noses full of powerful adhesive, are taking a well deserved break out front in the lilac-laden late spring air. It is a smoking break: they trade one lethal inhalant for another.

"Where are you from?" one asks us in broken English.

Minnesota, I say. New York State, says my IHE faculty colleague Mr. Angelos.

"How long have you been in Japan?" is the next question in a sequence that seems to be imprinted on the national DNA.

Ten months, I say. Just three, says Mr. Angelos.

The next question inevitably would be whether or not we like Japan, but just then two Japanese chicks saunter under the arched trellis. Like most of our live-in students, they are adorable and friendly, and greet us by name with singsong hellos.

One is Sato-san, a/k/a "Sugar," who attends a local college by day; the other is her seventeen-year-old roommate, known affectionately (though not very creatively) as Jailbait. As memory serves, each has a chirping bluebird perched on her shoulder, thus proving that memory cannot be trusted to serve.

Mr. Angelos and I have built up enough immunity to the spell of our friendly live-in Japanese chicks that we can respond politely. Not so the carpet-layers. These fellows clearly spend too much time in close corridors. It takes the disappearance of the chicks into the building to reanimate their drooping tongues.

"Excuse me," asks the elder through a parched throat, "but do you experience a good deal of satisfying sexual activity in this house?"[*]

"Why, yes. Yes, we do," I reply. "And yes, this is Heaven."

—◻—

But you have to earn your way into Heaven.

The Purgatory of my early days in Japan was the Venture Language School in downtown Osaka. Here we worked with businessmen one on one in ventilated closets.

We used the "direct method," which involved forty-minute lessons of intensive Q-and-A concerning small objects, thusly:

Teacher: Is this a pen?
Student: Yes, that is a pen.
Teacher: Is the pen red?
Student: No, the pen is not red.
Teacher: What color is the pen?
Student: The pen is blue.
Teacher: Are you a pen?
Student: No, I am not a pen.
Teacher: Am I a pen?
Student: No, you are not a pen.
Teacher: Am I bored?

---

[*] The actual wording was closer to "*You!... This house?...*" followed by the ferocious ramming of a thumb through a slit formed by the opposite thumb and index finger, a gesture that did not bode well for the gratification of Frau Carpet-layer.

Student: Yes, you are bored.
Teacher: Am I slowly inserting the pen in my rectum in some misguided attempt to stave off yet another psychotic episode in which I envision *myself* as a giant pen plunging in and out of the pulsating black heart of my supervisor, Mr. Katsuki?

— ◻ —

Those who observed my work, even the irksome Mr. Katsuki, accounted me "good at" the direct method. This, I thought was something akin to being good at exhaling, or at getting erections.

The direct method served the school well. It allowed for the hiring of young and callow "teachers" from the U.S. without any troublesome interviewing, since anyone could be trained to execute it competently.

It served us hirelings well, too, since we acquired visa status and entrée to Japan. Our immortal souls were not sold but merely held as collateral; we got them back at the end of a five-month contract.

So everyone made out like bandits at Venture Language School, except of course those who naively believed they could learn English there.

The boundless credulity of these young salaried men—and their then-world-beating employers who paid the tuition—was a thing to wonder at.

Once a week, I was asked to write an evaluation of a young banker or stockbroker whose contract was coming up for renewal. This task amounted to repeating the same basic message but with sufficient paraphrasing to prevent the student's personnel manager from wising up. The underlined words were substituted for, using a thesaurus.

Mr. <u>Nakamura</u> has attended his lessons <u>regularly</u> and made <u>significant</u> <u>efforts</u>. Thus, the <u>progress</u> in his English proficiency is marked. However, he has yet to attain a skill level sufficient for him to participate in business on an international stage. Further training is recommended.

The goal, usually achieved, was to induce said personnel manager to unlock the corporation's petty cash vault and haul out yet another wheelbarrow of yen notes to finance Mr. Nakamura's further instruction, until that golden day dawned when he would magically be capable of negotiating mergers and giving presentations at international colloquia in English.

In fact, no student ever left our little academe prepared to take part in any event but the Ninth International Symposium on Blue Pen Identification.

—◻—

I knew my days at Venture Language School were numbered when I met Mr. Yoshida.

He came to us in mid-June. The manufacturer for which he worked had selected him to go to Indonesia at the end of that month to hammer out a complicated import agreement with government officials there. With only half a month to prepare, he was compelled to take ten lessons a day. Our staff taught him by rotation, each of us in turn charmed by his genial, bubbly manner.

Alas, Mr. Yoshida began from a particularly low baseline. He stated firmly that he was, indeed, the blue pen and stood by this conviction, except on Fridays when, inexplicably, he became the phone.

When the time came to write Mr. Yoshida's midterm evaluation, I felt a need to break from form:

Mr. Yoshida has attended his lessons constantly and made Herculean efforts. His pleasant personality makes him easy to like and to work with. However, if he is sent abroad to conduct business in English only two weeks hence, he is doomed.

"What is this 'doomed'? What **does it** mean?" Mr. Katsuki asked me. The question was rhetorical, I felt, given that he was brandishing a bilingual dictionary over his outsized head. Before I could look up a mollifying synonym for doomed, he continued: "You cannot write 'doomed' in an evaluation!"

"But he *is* doomed."

"You must rewrite this evaluation!"

"No."

I am not usually so brusque in dealing with my superiors, but there were two factors at play here: First, Mr. Katsuki was tiny and powerless. A week earlier, one of my colleagues had threatened him with a metal folding chair and had suffered no consequences.

Second, both Mr. Katsuki and I knew that he would have his secretary retype the evaluation and forge my signature on it.

As for Mr. Yoshida, I'm fairly sure that he did indeed attend the business negotiations in Indonesia. I do not know the outcome. I am haunted by an image of the other kids taunting him, cruelly dialing numbers on his face.

—◻—

Later that summer, I was working on the present perfect tense with a young bespectacled executive one afternoon.

"Have you come to this school for many months?"

"Yes, I have come to this school for many months."

"How many months have you come to this school?"

"I have come to this school for... Excuse me. May I ask a question?"

Stunned by this *Matrix*-like awakening from the direct-method netherworld, I could not soon respond.

"Um, okay."

"What is the difference between 'I have come to the school' and 'I came to the school'?"

"Ah… Well… In the former case, you are still coming to the school. In the latter case, you *used* to come to the school, but you have stopped. You see?"

"No."

"Ah… Well…"

I had this zany idea. I picked up a chalk and wrote:

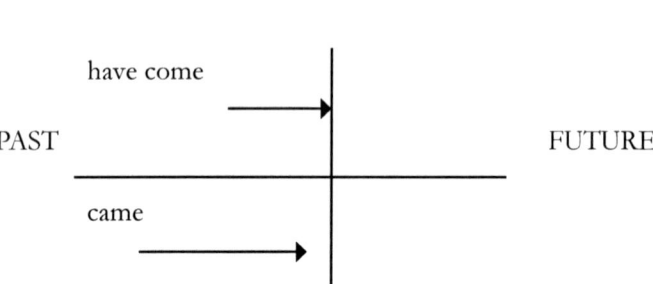

"So you see," said someone who sounded like me—a lad who only six months earlier had had to excuse himself from a private conference with his faculty advisor because the acid was kicking in sooner than expected and he was losing control over the impulse to remove the advisor's ears with a letter opener—"we use 'have come' to say that something began in the past and continues up to now. We use 'came' for something that finished *before* now."

The young executive mulled all this for a long moment. His head tilted back and his mouth flopped open. Something was happening here that was at once familiar and yet novel. I remember the moment clearly, even unto the way the late-afternoon sunlight poked through the narrow window and danced off his glasses as his head bobbed up and down.

HOW TO PICK UP JAPANESE CHICKS

"Ahh!" he said. "Ahh-ahh! *Ahh-AHHHH-ahh-ahh-ahh!!*"

It was an orgasm. No doubt about it. It was a *cerebral* orgasm. His brain *was coming*, present progressive tense.

It was the moment, the very instant, of learning. A tiny chunk of Ignorance had been displaced by Understanding just as, in an authentic orgasm, copious amounts of semen are displaced by...well, whatever it is that fills space when semen goes AWOL. Anyway, it was a great moment of satisfaction. It was, as they say, good for me too.

Damn, I am *good at this*, I realized. And I was hooked. For life.

—◻—

It was exciting to give a male Japanese executive a cerebral orgasm. But it made me all the more aware of my ongoing failure to give orgasms of any sort to Japanese chicks, or to receive the reciprocal gift from them.

In fact, Japanese chicks had "given" me plenty of orgasms by this time, in the manner that females from time immemorial have bestowed the gift of inspiration on young men, however unwittingly. Secretaries, the rare female Venture student, adjacent passengers on crowded commuter trains, even the Weird Sisters at Narita Airport had brought out the best in me. But none of them was ever physically present for the blessed event.

That had to change.

One day that long-ago summertime, a Venture colleague spoke of a magical place where the living is easy. Chicks are jumpin', and the cotton is high...

—◻—

Here's how you get to Heaven.

Halfway between the putrid urban anus called Osaka and the ancient capital Kyoto, the Daito commuter line stops at the suburb of Maezono.

Exiting from the east side, you are greeted by a sinister life-sized Ronald McDonald, permanently posed so as to point you in the right direction. Soon you reach a small pharmacy run by a man who, despite an unnerving resemblance to your old Sunday school teacher, is remarkably conversant on the subject of condoms. It is just past his shop that you zigzag onto the Street with No Sidewalk.

You will spend eight thrilling minutes dodging taxis on this street until you reach the liquor store, where you are always greeted like Caesar returning from the Gallic wars. Mr. Asai, a stalwart fellow capable of hoisting four cases of beer and of counting almost as high, may call out to inquire about your needs; and you just might have a pleasing answer for him.

You now turn onto an incline steeper and more tortuous than Big Thunder Mountain. This street also lacks sidewalks, and Olympic judges have chosen to add yet another degree of difficulty by placing open drainage ditches on both sides of it. When a car passes, the pedestrian is forced to step off the road and perch on the narrow ledge of the ditch, inhaling the aroma of rotting leaves marinated in the urine of impatient drunks.

Sweat-bathed after six more minutes of this trek, you reach a gravel driveway running off to the left, bounded by a mossy stone wall. Here, the incline becomes nearly perpendicular, though there is welcome shade from ancient cherry trees that sift the sun's severe rays into benevolent droplets.

Your goal is now at hand. You pass under the vine-bedecked iron trellis onto a brick walkway, auspicious sights that are mocked by the decaying monstrosity to which they lead.

"Barracks" would not be too harsh a word for the two-story twin wings that are bound together at the middle of the first floor where the common-use rooms are. The external walls are composed of some of extra-chromosome cousin of brownstone, which crumbles with alarming ease at one's touch. For appearances, the most prominent segment of outer wall has been covered with wood paneling painted in cheery blue and white stripes. Affixed white letters inform you that you have indeed arrived at the

INTERNATIONAL HOUSE OF ENGLISH

Below, a motto is likewise affixed to the wall in raised lettering. But weather has not been kind to it, gradually eroding it to

AL ATI NS ITE NDER O ROO

You rise to the *Wheel of Fortune* challenge:
"Dalmatians tonite plunder our rooms"?
"Alterations incite wonder of rookies"?
Oh, sorry panelists—time's up. The correct answer, Vanna?

ALL NATIONS UNITED UNDER ONE ROOF

The sentiment is a noble one. But when you first stepped inside the dank and musty *genkan* last summer, when you first felt the plywood flooring of the corridor sag under your feet, and later when you first felt the winter wind squeeze effortlessly around the window sash and crawl twixt layers of your futon, you were apt to suggest the more practical *Lord, just keep the leaky roof united—and over our heads one more night.*

This too has been one of the dark places of the earth, you may well have said—then. You took a room here last July for lack of other options and commuted to your job in the city. *It's just a port in the storm*, you told yourself—then.

But now this has been your home for nearly a year, and will be for one more. It has indeed been a dark place at times, but no building, no matter how dilapidated, flimsy, leaky, creaky, and likely to burst into a six-o-clock-news inferno at any moment, can be considered a truly dark place when it is blessed with such a luminous multitude of Japanese chicks.

—◘—

"It's high time we took English hours more seriously," warns a colorful magic-markered poster in the communal lounge.

"IHE" is an English immersion boarding school. Students of area colleges along with office workers in their twenties and thirties comprise the long-term populace. They pay exorbitant rents for the privilege of sleeping four to a room with little more personal space than passengers on the *Amistad*. Breakfast, dinner, and a nightly two-hour group lesson with a real live native-speaking teacher are included.

Profit-wise, the critical season is summer, when vacationing businessmen, retirees, and above all college-aged chicks, stream in from all over the country for six-hour-a-day intensive courses.

In the highly competitive world of commercial English education nothing is more critical than the dedication and rectitude of the live-in teaching staff.

—◘—

"I fucked that Tokiko chick last night," declares Fat Matt, slathering margarine on an encyclopedic slab of toast in the dining room one July morning, soon after I have moved in.

"She was so *light*. I just picked her up and hopped all over the room with her. First time I've done that. Ever try it? She let me spew inside her and everything. It was *great*."

—¤—

"Let me tell your fortune," Miki says, holding her deck of tarot cards.

"All right," I say. "But let's go to my room."

"Why not here?"

"There are all these people…" This is true. Evening classes let out at nine, so the lounge and adjoining dining room are now overflowing.

"So? Why do we have to go to your room?"

"I'm…a little shy about having my fortune read in front of everybody." This also is true, as far as it goes.

In the preceding ten days, Miki and I have been to a movie. We have attended an exotic festival in Kyoto in which huge portable shrines were hoisted down the street. We have lain in the grassy field outside the house and stared silently at the stars together. We have heard the chimes of…well, ten-thirty at least.

She is nineteen, a college student from that bowtie-shaped island. I am twenty-three.

She is short, thick-limbed—not displeasing to look at but too plain to entice Fat Matt and the other sundry chickivores who prowl the House. And I am, needless to say, desperate.

Like the many conquests loudly trumpeted by Fat Matt and his ilk, she is an intensive course student, in the House only for a two-week stay and, presumably, starving for cross-cultural contact of all sorts. And I, unlike Fat Matt and his ilk, am not employed as a teacher in the House.

We are just two rent-paying neighbors of legal age. And it is high time we took neighborly hospitality more seriously.

"Sorry, but it's the Room of Death," I say as I open the door.

"Pardon?"

"It's Room 4."

The word for "four" being a homophone of the word for "death," the number is often skipped in hotels and apartment buildings. But not in IHE.

The room is, in fact, little larger than a sumo wrestler's casket. Two-thirds of the floor space is consumed by the bed, the only furnishing to sit on. There is a tiny window and no air conditioning. For my hair, which has fallen out in dark, sweaty clumps the past few weeks, the nickname I have given the room is all too apt.

Miki begins laying down the cards on my small table and when she pauses, I, exercising the same judgment that told me the "Room of Death" crack would make a clever icebreaker, pull her down onto the mattress with me.

I expect one of the two customary reactions—intense resistance or contented acquiescence. That there is none of the former is instantly clear. But I am well into a unilateral French kiss and have laid claim to one handful of breast before it dawns on me that I am not getting the latter, either. Something is amiss…

I unbolt my face from hers but leave my hand entrenched to hedge my bet.

Sure enough, she is lying there fixing me with the glazed, unblinking stare of a corpse.

"Why are you doing this?"

Good question. I cease groping her, the better to grope for an answer. But I come up empty-handed all around.

"I think you are lonely," she says, in the vaguely sad tone of a fast-food clerk stating that it is now too late to order the breakfast menu.

I deny loneliness as a motive but, unable to hit on a plausible alternative, I retreat.

Miki calmly resumes the tarot card reading. Whatever her prognostication turns out to be, the words "You'll get lucky tonight" will not occur in it.

Lord, I pray, *you may now disregard previous requests re keeping the roof from falling on our heads.*

—◻—

Two weeks later, with Miki long gone back to Bowtie Island, the House sponsors an overnight outing to nearby Lake Biwa.

I am riding in the back of a small pickup truck with a freshly hatched batch of intensive-course chicks. Morning sunbeams flirt with us through the cedars and the scented breeze caresses our cheeks, and all is right with the world.

—◻—

I have a few photos taken in the late afternoon, not long after our arrival.

On the sandy lakeshore we have set up the tents and prepped the barbecue grills under the jolly guidance of Mr. Naito, a mature-beyond-his-years college boy who works as assistant manager in the office. The four o'clock beer in his hand, the grin on his broad face, the colossally embarrassing plaid Bermuda shorts on his broader butt all belie his status as the chaperone of this event.

Meanwhile, I have changed into my swimsuit, and pose with House chicks in theirs.

—◻—

I am swimming through the silty murk to a large anchored raft. Several of us congregate there, swiftly drying in the warm lake-wind. The dudes, naturally, soon find themselves running out of conversation topics and take to grabbing chicks and hurling them into the lake.

The chicks put up the universal shrieking resistance to the prospect of getting wet, though none of them teleported to the raft. The soft summer air is crackling with animal energy.

As the lake trip was a spontaneous plan, several participants have come without swimsuits. They have plunged into the lake in their regular clothes. One of these is Atsuko, just out of high school and gorgeous. Atsuko is unaware that the magic waters of Lake Biwa have rendered her t-shirt and bra almost totally transparent. The dudes, myself included, are most keenly aware.

We return to shore. The scent of grilled beef and vegetables fills the air, and one appetite is momentarily shoved aside in favor of another. The males wash down the meal with beer, the females—apart from my burly no-nonsense neighbor, Susan the Australian—with soft drinks.

— ¤ —

Weirdly, there is an illuminated stage complete with karaoke machine within projectile-vomiting distance of our campsite, and several small round tables are lodged in the sand around it. Our group quickly monopolizes this rustic little slice of Vegas as night falls.

Liquored-up males take to the stage one by one to warble through the usual overwrought *enka* ballads in a misguided attempt to impress chicks. (The chicks politely applaud, fueling the flames.) Out of the blue someone produces a bottle of Canadian Club, the favored elixir of my college days. Just the antidote for tenor toxicity, I am sure.

Mr. Naito is roaming the floor, trying in vain to get the foreigners into the act. Even here, *sans* roof, he wants All Nations United.

"But I don't know any *enka* songs."

"Well, just go up and sing something."

I take the stage to riotous applause. I slur a needless self-introduction and launch into an *a cappella* rendition of Jerry Jeff Walker's "London Homesick Blues." The crowd picks up the beat and claps along.

This has a Tinkerbell-like effect. I finish to thunderous huzzahs. I am a tough act to follow, though this does not at all impede several repeat offenders from reclaiming the stage.

I am summoned by Mr. Naito to another table, where he has thoughtfully brought my whiskey and—even better—Atsuko. Her clothes have now dried, enabling me to look her in the eyes. These, too, are a nicely matched pair.

"You sing very well," she says.

"She likes you a lot," Mr. Naito says.

Atsuko slaps Mr. Naito on the shoulder.

"Do you like me?" I manage to articulate.

"Yes…I like you."

"I love you."

This marks the first of two thousand four hundred and eighty-two times and counting that I have uttered this sentence to a Japanese chick and actually meant it. It also marks my last coherent sentence of the weekend. The rest is jangling participles.

—◻—

Predawn light. The karaoke-like caterwauling of whatever insensitive birds populate the Lake Biwa ecosystem.

Telegrams pouring in from the body's remote precincts: *Urination now, urination forever!*

Staggering out of the Venusian atmosphere of the men's tent, finding some bushes for cover. The relief of bladder pressure.

The gradual regrouping of beleaguered brain cells who have survived yet another attempted genocide. Let the internal war crimes trial begin:

Brain Cell 1: The horror, the horror…

Brain Cell 2: We did it again. Oh boy, did we do it this time.

Brain Cell 3: I am a memory cell. I refuse to die before I tell my tale.

Brain Cell 4: Oh, tell it! Tell it!

Brain Cell 3: We were in the girls' tent last night.

Brain Cell 1: How? Why?

Brain Cell 3: How? By crawling under a loose flap. Why? Do you ask me "why"? Do you not remember Atsuko?

Brain Cell 5: And? And?

Brain Cell 3: Trial and error, bro. Rolling one chick over and stunning her awake with the foulness of our breath to see if she was Atsuko. Or, if not Atsuko, then anyone acceptable.

Brain Cell 4: Acceptable for what?

Brain Cell 3: A thing without a name…

Brain Cell 2: And then?

Brain Cell 3: And then rolling over another chick, and another. Then there was squealing, shrieking, a crescendo of female distress… There was ear-dragging…

Brain Cell 4: "Ear-dragging"?

Brain Cell 3: Susan the Australian. She took possession of our ear.

Brain Cell 2: Did we fail to keep up the payments?

Brain Cell 5: Ha-ha. Good one, Two!

Brain Cell 3: I grow dim… We are being dragged back to the male tent… Being told "Stay!"

Me: Enough—

Brain Cell 3: Clambering over our bloated tent-mates as they groan and fart and curse us—

Me: Enough! Enough!

Brain Cell 3: There might be more… Can't…hold…on…

Brain Cell 2: Hang in there, Three!

Brain Cell 3: Seen…too…much…

—◻—

I peek toward both tents. No sign of life.

I stagger down the beach past the tents of other weekend campers. I follow the curve of the shore until out of sight of my housemates.

I find a boulder embedded in the beach. I perch on top of it when slithering under it proves unfeasible.

I sit there on that stony throne as the blistering sun rises over me; as the mocking laughter of waking children engulfs me; as I lapse in and out of consciousness, each time hoping to awaken into a parallel dimension in which I am a much finer person but each time finding myself just a more dehydrated one; as I dimly realize that somewhere around the bend my Housemates too are awakening and accounts of the night's vile events are being shared and compared; as I realize that sooner or later, dead or alive, I will be found.

—◻—

It is Mr. Naito who comes upon my shriveled husk.

In an earlier, nobler era, he would have quietly placed a dagger in my hand and toddled away, granting me the honor of disemboweling myself in the shadow of my rock.

But I cannot expect so much kindness. Instead, I expect him to say, "You will, of course, pack your bags as soon as we return to the House."

His tone is quite different.

"Josh-san. What are you doing here?"

"I wanted to be alone."

"We're having breakfast now."

"I'm not really hungry."

"I think it would make you feel better."

"I doubt that."

My stony throne can accommodate two. Mr. Naito's Bermuda-themed butt pours onto the adjacent space.

I recall our first meeting in the IHE office on the day of my arrival: *My name sounds like 'night-o,' but I'm the day manager!*

The very word *night* brings agony now. I do not want to live to see another night, nor talk with a man of that name.

"There are always a lot of girls at IHE," he is saying.

I know where this is going, and I know better than to speak.

"A lot of pretty girls… They make us crazy sometimes."

We look at the lake in silence for a while.

"You know, we *all* get a little too crazy sometimes."

"I think I just want to sit here for a while," I say, and the sound of my voice confirms my suspicion that Mr. Naito's words have brought me very near to tears.

He nods and rises. "We'll be leaving in about an hour. Come back when you're ready."

—◻—

I go into exile at the YMCA in the city. I hold out for a week.

Only smiling faces greet me when I return. Atsuko and any other likely victims have departed. A new intensive course group has taken over the house.

The other male foreigners inquire about my absence, but I remain vague. They arrive at their own consensus, thus voiced by Fat Matt:

"You've been getting some pussy, haven't you?"

"Well, I—"

"Shacking up with some chick? Somebody from that school you work at?"

"I've, uh, been in the city."

"Yeah, well, good for you. It's about fuckin' time, man!"

—◻—

Exile is over, but penance not yet served.

I forswear alcohol for a month, and hold to it.

I make no overt advances on House chicks—or Japanese chicks of any other subspecies, for that matter.

I vow to become the Watcher. Like the Marvel Comics character, I will passively observe and record human activity. Unlike him, I will refrain from making tut-tutting comments on humanity's failings, for obvious reasons.

Watch, listen, and learn the lessons…

—◻—

> *Teaching Point 2: You are not alone.*

A barbecue party is held the weekend after Biwagate in the open field next to the house. An unknown foreigner appears. He introduces himself as a former resident.

"Lived here for two years," he says. "Naito-san called me up and told me about the party."

"So what do you do now?"

He names a renowned English school chain. "Pretty good money," he says.

A few intensive course chicks flutter over and grace us with a few minutes of rudimentary, titter-laced conversation.

"It never changes. Is this a great place to live, or what?"

"Yep."

"Did I hear you say you've got Room Four?"

"Yep."

"The Room of Death, eh? That was my room, too. Don't you, like, have to run up there about three times every day and whack off like a monkey?"

"Yep."

He is reading my mind like an open pamphlet.

"I know *I* did."

That explains the carpeting, I think but do not say.

—◻—

> *Teaching Point 3: Your fur is not your friend. Evolve, or cover.*

As the communal bathrooms are in the opposite wing of the House, my most direct route from the Room of Death takes me through the centrally located lounge and dining area. Feeling more at home now, I take to making this journey wearing only my U of M gym shorts—and make a point of doing so at the peak social hour in the lounge, just after evening classes have let out.

My near-naked forays bring an inevitable cascade of what I assume to be appreciative tittering. Like many a five-nine gaijin, I am experiencing the joy of walking tall for the first time in my life.

I flaunt my Conneryesque chest forestation and equally macho legs. Surely Japanese chicks are comparing me favorably to my shorter, eerily hairless Japanese rivals.

One night I stop to chat with some chicks at the dining room table so as to allow them a better view. Etsuko, a long-term resident nearing the upper parameter of chickhood, speaks for the group.

"Josh-san, your body is so hairy."

"Thank you. Thank you very much."

"I mean, your body is *very* hairy."

"Yes, yes!"

"Very, *very hairy.*"

"Ah…"

To this day, even in the privacy of my home, I head for the shower dressed like the bride at a Wahhabi wedding.

— ¤ —

Teaching Point 4: A rise in success is a function of a drop in expectations.

There is this shadowy figure known as Arthur who rarely ventures far from his room. He is the Boo Radley of IHE. Pallid, scrawny, stoop-shouldered and shy, he shatters the stereotype of a So-Cal boy.

His only sales points besides his gaijin-ness are a distinct lack of hair anywhere below the eyebrows and an utter lack of shame in any aspect of his being. Those, plus a room, for some reason, in the predominantly female wing of the house.

Purely by batting average, Arthur is the most successful male in IHE history. But then, he swings only at the fattest and laziest pitches.

Arthur's clients are those female residents who are invisible to the rest of us, existing well outside the chick spectrum. He chooses the dowdy, the pimply, the halt, the lame, the self-loathing, the inarticulate, the keening mastiffs yearning to drink tea.

Tea, not tarot, is Arthur's MacGuffin. He keeps a hotplate in his room and invites his marks to enjoy his special blend.

Arthur's room is separated from his neighbor's by a thin partition that allows sound to pass freely. The neighbor, of necessity a heavy drinker, recounts a typical Arthur seduction session thusly:

Arthur: How's your tea?
Pimply girl: Oon?
Arthur: Your tea. How is it?
Pimply girl: Ehh?
Arthur: Would you like a little more?
Pimply girl: Wakannai.
Arthur: More…tea?
Pimply girl: Oh… No thank you.
Arthur: You know, I really like you.
Pimply girl: Oon?
Arthur: Here…
Pimply girl: Oon??
Arthur: Sssssss… Mmmmmm…
Pimply girl: Ehhh?? Hahhhh???
Arthur: Mmmmmmfffff….
Pimply girl: Ohhhhh…
[Miscellaneous slurps, gasps, hoots, moos, gobbles and grunts; fade to black.]

A serial monogamist, Arthur sticks with one unblessed partner for as long as she resides in the house. Upon her departure, he lapses into a silent funk for about a week.

Then, it's time to fire up the teapot again.

—¤—

> *Teaching Point 5: Learn the native words, or at least how to fake it.*

Fat Matt is fat. And obnoxious. And ugly. And fat. He doesn't smell so great, either. He is boastful and pigheaded. And let it not be forgotten that he is, in no small part, fat.

But he speaks Japanese of a sort. Though he speaks it poorly, he speaks it better than I do, and I despise him for it. I envy him mainly for his brazenness in thundering out his horrid grammar. This generates laughter from Japanese chicks, and a laughing-at-the-kitchen-table Japanese chick is much more likely to become a doing-naked-jumping-jacks-in-your-room Japanese chick. Fat Matt knew this by instinct.

I take the quieter approach to the language by studying reading and writing. I set about mastering the native alphabet of forty-six characters which can be used to express any word phonetically.

As with the English alphabet, high-frequency letters tend to appear near the beginning while some of those near the end are rarely used. Thus, just as a small American child may possess a vocabulary that jarringly includes a whopper like *xylophone* or *X-ray* along with *apple*, *ball*, and *cat*, I am soon in command of a fifty-odd-word Japanese vocabulary that includes *man*, *chair*, and *leprosy*. On a good day, I can even write complete sentences like "The man in the chair has leprosy," or "The man's leprosy is under the chair."

I make a point of sitting in the lounge, conspicuously poring over my workbook. Kind Japanese chicks are drawn to my chair like tornados to a trailer park. They revel in quizzing me on characters and words. I revel in sitting really, really close to kind Japanese chicks.

—◘—

Over time, I develop a reputation in the House as White Man Who Tries to Learn Our Words.

I earn the title by default. Apart from Fat Matt, nobody really makes an effort. As long as chicks can be won over with tea, what's the point? Roelof, the English teacher from South Africa, speaks no Japanese and is still working on intelligible English, but it doesn't slow him down.

One Sunday morning, I am out behind the house manually transferring my laundry into the spin drier when one of life's too-good-to-be-true coincidences strikes. God sends me a young man—not for my sexual pleasure or even to help with my laundry, but for a rarer purpose.

"Josh-san, I have a question. I don't know if you can help me."

"What is it?"

"How do you say *rai-byo* in English?"

"Oh, that. It's leprosy."

"Ah! Thank you!"

It's all coasting after that. I become the Keanu Reeves of Japanese fluency.

—◘—

> *Teaching Point 6: Don't believe your own press clippings.*

"It is a great pleasure to meet you at last, Muggins-san," said Mr. Wakamatsu, shooting up from his chair and pumping my hand. "Mr. Naito has told me of your need for a new visa sponsor. It will be taken care of. I've heard many good things about you!" he continued. And then he died.

Not right then and there in the International House of English office. Our mysterious owner and founder had three more good solid months of life in him before expiring of kidney failure after yet another vigorous evening of drinking and whoring. He was thirty-five.

Mr. Wakamatsu's first words to me (and last words, as it turned out) struck an odd chord, seeing as I had by that time committed possibly actionable sexual assault on three or four of his paying customers. True, I had kept my nose clean for two straight weeks, but still, you would think.

I thanked Mr. Wakamatsu for his no-strings-attached offer. Visa sponsorship would free me to pick from a smorgasbord of better paying part-time jobs in the city now that my Venture contract was ending.

My doomed sponsor cocked an eyebrow at me. I looked to Mr. Naito. He replied with a shrug. So much for the "no strings attached" angle. I suddenly felt like a POW in a black-and-white war movie.

We have ways of making you teach.
Oh, well…

On weekends, the intensive course students, who come from remote areas of Japan, always want to tour the traditional cities of Kyoto and Nara, and seek to share the joy of discovery with the newest IHE faculty member. I am happy to rise early on Sunday mornings and discover the Temple of the Golden Pavilion, Kiyomizu Temple, the Deer Park of Nara, the Giant Buddha of Todaiji and many others.

As the intensive course students turn over week by week, I find myself sharing the joy of these discoveries time and again with each new group. To girlfriends who think that faking a convincing orgasm is troublesome, I propose the challenge of faking amazement at the "chirping cypress flooring" of Nijo Castle the sixth time you have trod upon it.

There are afternoon tea parties with these chick-laden intensive groups. There are disco-dancing farewell parties in the lounge and barbecue parties in the field. I dutifully attend all events, and dutifully keep my hands to myself—about three times a day up in the Room of Death, just as my predecessor had.

Whatever scarlet letter may have been branded on me after Biwagate has vanished. Chicks cluster around me. Still, I cannot be sure if it is safe to make a move. The YMCA was no fun at all. I need a Sign from God.

One day, I receive a fan letter! From a girl named Tomoe, a former intensive course chick! I cannot place her face, even with the aid of the enclosed group photo of her class. But surely she adores me.

Dear Josh-sensei,

How are you! I'm fine. Two weeks have passed since I left IHE. Now I am back in Tokyo. My college life will begin again soon!

The time that we spent together at IHE was very precious for me. I thank you from the bottom of my heart! It was the most significant time of my life! You are a very kind teacher! I was so happy to meet you and talk with you!! I am yearning to meet you again someday!!!

I enclose a photo which was taken at our farewell party!! Please don't forget me forever!!!!!!

Sincerely,
Tomoe

Is this not a cry for help? Vow of celibacy or no, can I, in good conscience, just sit here in Osaka while the poor girl wastes away in Tokyo, yearning to meet me? Just how soon can I get vacation time to go to Tokyo? When does the next train leave?

I stagger out of my room and immediately bump into Roelof, squinting fiercely into a piece of familiar flowery blue stationery. The script on that stationery is likewise familiar, down to the precise distribution of exclamation points.

"Roelof. I…I got exactly the same letter."

"Yah. Matt gawt wun, tew."

"Ah…"

"Wudda weerd cheek, eh?"

—◻—

> *Teaching Point 7: There* is *a limit.*

A few weeks after the passing of her husband, the young Widow Wakamatsu takes a call on the office phone. Remarkably enough, someone wants Arthur.

Not yet familiar with House etiquette, the Widow opens the door to Arthur's room without knocking and has her fragile psyche scorched with the image of Arthur and a bovine student making wild, passionate tea.

Arthur receives one week's notice.

—◻—

On one of his last nights before eternal banishment, I would find Arthur out back, beyond the laundry poles, at the edge of the cliff. It was not a cliff off which one could plunge into blissful oblivion, merely the sort off which one could plunge into assorted scrapes, bruises and regrets. So I did not fear for his safety.

Few words had ever passed between us, but on this night he was as expansive as the torsos of many of his consorts.

"I'm sorry that you're leaving, Arthur. What are you going to do?"

"I don't know. I guess I'll go back to San Diego."

"Can't you stay? In Japan, I mean."

"Her parents are threatening to call Immigration."

"Oh."

"You know, it wasn't just... You know? Not just *that*. I really *liked* that girl."

He sighed and added:

"I really liked *all* of them."

I did not know what to say to him, so I simply joined him in staring off into the broad, speckled suburban sky. It was a chilling, moving moment, or at least would have been had we not been standing directly atop the House septic tank.

Were there another chance, I suppose I would say, "I'm sure they all liked you, too, Arthur."

LESSON 3

Be used and discarded like a mindless tool, and learn to love it

...but for sweet Jack Falstaff, kind Jack Falstaff, true Jack Falstaff, valiant Jack Falstaff, banish not him thy Harry's company: banish plump Jack, and banish all the world.

—*Henry IV, Part One*

Owwwwww! Ow, ow! Owwwwwwww!

—Numerous Japanese actresses in numerous theatrically released pornographic films

It is hard now to recall an era when one viewed filmed sex acts with a roomful of strangers.

Unless you were one of those patrons with no sense of decency or qualms about littering, you were forced to compile an elaborate memory file which could be downloaded in the privacy of your room some hours later. Damned inconvenient. A tale to make the grandkids marvel someday.

"What did you think of that?" Jiro asked me.

"The girls were pretty, but…"

"What?"

"They just didn't seem to be having much fun."

True that. While one does not expect a great deal of exposition in an adult film, a little preliminary banter to assure us that the participants have come to their profession willingly is but little to ask for. Late seventies Japanese porn stars exuded notably less *joie de vivre* at work than did the average carpet layer.

Yet no matter how crummy the movie, it was ever worth the price of admission to point at Jiro as we exited the theater and proclaim to the street at large, *"This man is a high school teacher! A teacher of innocent girls here, coming out of a filthy movie!"*

—◻—

Jiro came into my life as a member of a two-week summer intensive course cohort. An Osaka native, he often called me that autumn to arrange outings on weekends.

It was he who kindly introduced me to various forms of Japanese cuisine, to the primordial video games of the era, and to even more plebeian art forms.

In time I came to suspect that Jiro was using me. At twenty-seven he was still living at home, as most unmarried Japanese do, and saving his meager salary toward entrance to an American graduate school so that he might one day become a professor of American literature. My role in this scheme was to allow him to practice English on the cheap.

Nonetheless, I enjoyed my weekends with him. He was the closest thing to a real friend that I had and hands down my finest pimp ever. For Jiro knew well that another handy application of the prototypical Young Foreign Friend was as bait to lure chicks who otherwise would not come within fly-casting range.

He invited Yachiyo along for a September picnic in Kyoto. She was another area resident who had been in his intensive group—one of the many who had tutored me in the *katakana* alphabet. She was a grand master of the pseudo-modest hand-cloaked titter. Among my several photos of her, only one includes her lower face.

Jiro had the bright idea to rent a rowboat for a romantic cruise along the broad river at Arashiyama. It was indeed romantic for Yachiyo and me, who sat in the back of the boat flirting and tittering and reminiscing about those halcyon days of four weeks earlier, while Jiro rowed. Yachiyo gave me her phone number unsolicited. We began to date.

—◻—

"Teach me some bad words in English."
"Hmm, let's see. You know this one?"

I wrote the F word on a coffee shop napkin.

"Yes, I know."

"Okay, what else…"

"What do you call this?"

"Oh, uh, those would be *tits*. Usually plural."

The napkin continued to serve as a substitute blackboard.

"That's sort of a man's word, though," I continued. "Girls are more likely to call them *boobs*."

"*Boobs*. That's funny!"

"Yes, isn't it. Let's see. This fellow right here is a, er, well, this word."

"*Coke*."

"Better open the mouth a little more."

"*Co-o-ock*."

"Yes, much better."

"*Co-o-ock*."

"Oh, you're doing great… Then the one that *you* have, why, we would call that…"

"*Pussy*."

"Uh-huh. Splendid. Shall we, uh, review?"

"Are there more bad words?"

"Hmm… Well, do you know this one?"

"*Ash-hole*."

"It's pronounced *ass-hole*, actually."

"What is it?"

"Well, most often it just means a bad person or a stupid person. Do you remember Fat Matt from the House?"

"Oh, yes!"

"Okay. He's an asshole."

"Ah. It's like *baka* in Japanese?"

"Yes, yes. But it also means a part of your body. Down here."

"I thought it's *butt*."

"Well, the general *area* is called *butt* or *ass*. But you see, there's a hole in there."

"Ahh."

"Right about here. That's called the assho—"

"Oh, it's getting late. I have to go back now."

> *Teaching Point 8: When teaching naughty words to a Japanese chick, start at the top and stop at the ones that apply mainly to heterosexual activity.*

—◻—

Dates with Yachiyo had to begin around lunchtime. She was obliged to be home by early evening at the latest, lest she face an inquiry. Her parents could not know that she was seeing a foreigner (see *The State vs. Arthur*, etc.).

I sought to optimize these narrow windows of time.

"Say, why don't you come back out to Maezono this Saturday?"

"What for?"

"Well… There's a new *okonomiyaki* restaurant that's really good… And you could come and see the House again!"

"No, thank you. Let's meet in the usual place."

—◻—

So we would meet in Shinsaibashi, the entertainment district of Osaka.

We would have lunch, see a movie, and if the mood was right, have coffee or go for a walk afterward.

Sometimes I doomed a date from the start. The selection of English films was limited, and I would make the common male blunder of suggesting something that I wanted to see rather than something that would set a proper ambiance. My most egregious such error was *Invasion of the Body Snatchers*, the seventies remake. It was an effort to keep her from fleeing for home before the credits rolled on that one.

> *Teaching Point 9: Eschew "date movies" that feature tentacle-spewing pods, a creature with a man's face and a bulldog's body, eerie walking zombies, and (excuse the redundancy) Donald Sutherland.*

Yet, there were also those occasions when all seemed right with the world. The movie would prove blandly entertaining and would let us out with plenty of time to spare. We would pause to savor a breeze over the Dotonbori bridge and chat about her dreams of becoming a flight attendant.

There was expectation in her eyes, but I had no clue how to meet it. *Because nobody had told me about love hotels!*

Why hadn't anybody told me about love hotels?? And why had I not thought to ask?

I had segued all too smoothly from the college world of dorm- or apartment-based sex into IHE's parallel milieu. It never occurred to me that the country-western concept of unseemly meetings at pay-by-the-hour motels could apply anywhere in the world beyond a thousand-mile radius of Nashville. And yet, this was The Rule in Japan.

I had seen them. They were forthrightly labeled "love hotels."[*] They were tucked away on side-streets, but their signboards could be glimpsed from main thoroughfares. Much too late, I could recall Yachiyo leading me into areas of their heaviest concentration on our seemingly aimless strolls.

Damn me! Damn me! Damn me!!

---

[*] Written in Japanese characters as "rabu hoteru," which could be rendered back into English as "love hotel," "lab hotel," or "rub hotel." For any couples who performed like those I had watched in adult films with Jiro, either of the latter two readings would serve.

> *Teaching Point 10: When in Rome, promptly find out where the Romans go to copulate.*

—▫—

Banishment was inevitable. Yachiyo gave up on me but Jiro, bless his soul, did not.

For my twenty-fourth birthday in October, he gave me three tarted-up juniors from his alma mater.

How he came up with them, I know not. He still worked as a volunteer advisor for the school's English study club, but these chicks were not members. Their only obvious club affiliation was the Chicks-Who-Want-Nothing-To-Do-With-Jiro-Unless-He-Can-Dig-Up-A-Real-Live-Foreigner Club.

Two of them spoke no English, but the third more than compensated. By this stage of my stay, I had lapsed into gaijin-speak, the tendency to over-ar-ti-cu-late... e-ve-ry.... wo-o-ord. I was in training for the verbal marathon, but Motoko was running sprints.

Where are you from? What made you come to Japan? Are you interested in Japanese culture? You've read Mishima? In translation? What did you think of it? Oh, you just didn't get it—it's supposed to be homoerotic! How come you talk so funny?

We were touring temples of Nara that day. Jiro had actually found some that I had not yet been dragged to by intensive course students. But Motoko had me so dazzled from the get-go that we could just as well have been touring the canals of Mars.

I tried to speak to the other two, if only for a respite:

"My, Kazuyo, you sure have a lot of jewelry. Are those real pearls?"

But we needed Motoko to interpret.

"Yes, they are," said Motoko, channeling Kazuyo. "And see this ring? That's a real sapphire. It cost two hundred thousand yen. It's a present from her lover."

"You mean 'boyfriend'," I said, seeking at least to reclaim supremacy in my own language.

"No, her lover. He's a dentist with two kids. Her boyfriend doesn't know about that."

"Well, let's try to keep it among ourselves, then."

—◻—

Come nightfall, the chicks wanted to go to a disco in the Umeda district of Osaka.

I loathed disco and had proudly abstained from all efforts to make me dance when the craze finally reached Minnesota circa seventy-seven. But by this point in the day, I would have cheerfully joined Motoko in a rousing evening of cow-tipping or a papal-assassination scheme.

A huge mirror backed the dance floor. Dancers stood in rows and columns facing it. Dancing with a partner—even *having* a partner—was verboten. We looked like the Touretter High School Marching Band. I sidled close enough to Motoko to do The Bump with her. The icy stares of our fellow dancers branded us subversives.

She gave me her phone number and insisted that I call.

—◻—

By the time we arranged our first date, I had taken Love Hotel 101 courtesy of the more worldly lads at the House. Now the only problem was where to take her on the date itself. She would not see a movie with me, so I was stumped. I let her choose the venue.

She chose a bar—dark, quiet, decorated with fifties American movie posters (James Dean, Marilyn Monroe), American in every way but the prices.

There was no need for me to plan topics of conversation, as Motoko immediately resumed her role as inquisitor. I was astounded to realize that everything I believed—indeed, everything I even believed I believed—was wrong.

"What about this hostage crisis in Iran?"

"As an American, of course I'm upset about it."

"What are you, some kind of super-patriot?"

"No, not at all. I know my government does awful things in the world."

"Like what?"

"Um, Vietnam. My friends and I were totally against that. And…and the CIA interference in Chile, in Cuba and so on."

"The CIA interfered in Iran, too, you know. It was the CIA who put in the Shah in the first place."

"Well…yes… But that was twenty-five years ago. I mean, get over it."

"Is there some sort of statute of limitations on justice?"

"Well…yeah. I guess…" *Statute of limitations?* My Lord…

"What would it be, then? Ten years? Twenty?"

"Would you like to go for a walk?"

A hopeful pause. Then a glance at her watch, which I noticed was far too expensive and elegant to have been purchased by a university student.

"The last train is coming in fifteen minutes."

Damn these efficient Japanese trains.

"Okay. Well, there's a Christmas party at our House in Maezono on the twenty-second. May I escort you to it?"

"I won't know anybody there."

"You'll know me."

"I guess it's okay."

Motoko wore a cobalt-blue satiny number to the party. She was absurdly overdressed for an IHE function. I didn't mind; the attention she drew was most gratifying.

The subsequent undressing in the cupboard-like Room of Death, however, was a military operation. This despite the fact that, for the first time, I had a Japanese chick cooperating in her undressing.

She wore a slip under her dress. I had never seen one on a female of my own generation before. For a ghastly moment, I saw Mom getting dressed for bridge club. I shunned that image. Down that road, madness lay.

She didn't smell like Mom. She sure didn't kiss like Mom. And as the excavation through strata of underthings progressed, oh, what splendid un-Mom-like museum pieces did we unearth.

Her nipples were surprisingly tiny: two taut little red spots on twin moons whose stimulation brought immediate pleasure to both of us. It was clear from the start that Planet Motoko was highly seismic from pole to pole, a hot and noisy young world.

I had my own subterranean rumblings to consider. Motoko seized me in her tiny hands, like two eight-year-olds trying to determine which team would bat first. But I knew that this game would be rained out before it got underway unless I used a delaying tactic.

As I embarked south of the equator (slipping back into the geophysical metaphor here), there was some token resistance, soon overcome.

"*Aaaaiiiiiiioooooooo!*" she cried, pausing to add "*Ohhhhhh-wooooo-wahhhhhhhh!*"

She continued to inventory all vowels and diphthongs in the English language, including some that can only be rendered in the International Phonetic Alphabet.*

Soon, she was wriggling upward, whipping her neck from side to side and producing more decibels than all the combined sexual encounters of my college career.

I kept pace, tongue ever extended lest I lose my place, like a bloodhound on a very slow pursuit. The next day, I would find severe carpet burns on my knees and elbows that I could not at first account for.

Soon Motoko ran out of wriggling room on the floor and launched a physics-defying ascent of the wall. I wondered, momentarily, where in suburban Osaka Prefecture I would find an exorcist who made midnight house calls.

When she reached a full standing posture, she closed off the access. Catching her breath, she lay down again and beckoned for the main event.

The stalling tactic had served its purpose, and I was able to give her a full hour of thrusting pleasure!† At the moment of critical mass, I realized that it was a bit late for our chat about birth control.

I fleetingly recalled a kitchen-table conference among the gaijin males in which I had asked the old hands about the use of condoms.

"Not a problem. Japanese girls just don't get pregnant."

"Ay. Dey dawnt gitt prignunt."

That seemed questionable. And yet Motoko herself had invited me in without any cautions or instructions—at least, none that contained consonants.

At that stage, all I could do was make an announcement and try to gauge the response.

"I'm coming," I said.

---

* For which I do not have the proper font.
† All right, all right. I'm guessing 1.5 minutes. Yes, there is a decimal point in there.

There was a detectable curling of her eyebrows at this news. Whether the expression meant "No you don't!" or "But you're already here," I would never know. Anyway, the spermatozoa mob was already fleeing its cells in what was surely the greatest mass escape in the history of my scrotum.

Somebody was spewing vowel sounds not known outside the Hindi-Urdu language family. *"Waaaaw-hyoooooo!"*

Hindi-Urdu by way of Yosemite Sam.

—◻—

She blew off my next few efforts to ask her out.

The prying of the other foreigners didn't help. "You seeing much of that girlfriend of yours?" Fat Matt would ask, and then add, "The one with the tits, I mean," so as to distinguish her from my bountiful reserve of titless girlfriends.

Finally, she called me. She was meeting a few girl friends from high school for dinner and drinks down in Kobe, and they wanted to meet me.

Kobe was so far, I protested. If we could get a hotel room down there and stay over, I'd gladly do it. She agreed.

—◻—

We checked into a "business hotel" that Motoko had reserved and taxied to a *kaiseki ryori* restaurant. She declined comment on the fresh pack of condoms I gleefully flashed as if they had magically appeared in my jacket pocket. We were running late and had no time for such nonsense.

We were led through sliding *shoji* into a private *tatami* room. On one side of the table sat Motoko's two high school classmates. On the other side were three males. They were as surprised to see me as I to see them.

Motoko knew one of the males, though none of them were high school classmates. Two of them, I gleaned, were in training to become airline pilots.

The talk was rapid-fire, whiskey-fueled and in Japanese. Yet it was not exactly jovial, nor sexually charged in any way that I could discern. It was turgid, like the exposition in a Japanese porn film. Not a good sign.

I sat next to Motoko on the "girls' side." She made a few efforts to bring me into the conversation, but the other males weren't biting. My Japanese studies had fossilized, and no one wanted to discuss leprotic men or their chairs, so I was left out.

About two hours into the largely liquid meal, I mentioned that I felt a bit ill and wanted to go back to the hotel to lie down. This, of course, was but a clever ruse! An unmistakable signal to Motoko that it was time for us to go!

"Oh, that's too bad," she said.

"I'm not sure how to get back to the hotel."

The males, Kobe natives, knew. Motoko instructed them to take me a few blocks and point the way.

"I'll be back soon," she said as the *shoji* slid shut, but she wasn't.

—◻—

That spring, I received a short but cheery letter:

Dear Josh,

I have good news! I have been accepted as a flight attendant by Japan Airlines. I stay in Tokyo now to begin the training.

Thank you very much for teaching me English. I owe my good news to you!

Love,
Yachiyo

An expanse of white space remains below the closing. If I wave the letter over a flame, I'm fairly certain that the following addendum, written in lemon juice, will appear:

When you glimpse me through the curtain as I chat cheerfully with wealthy men in first class, always remember that you could have had me as often as you liked in any position that your warped mind could devise, if you had only taken the time to learn our customs.
Ha, ha, ha, ha, ha!
You asshole.

—◻︎—

Some months later, I received another letter.

Dear Josh,

I'm in Colorado now! I have to take a semester of undergraduate courses, and then I can begin my master's degree.

It's hard, but I'm getting used to it. The weather here is very cold, even though it's October.

Thanks for everything. I could enter this university owing to your kindness.

Regards,
Jiro

I do not think there was any ghostwriting on Jiro's letter. I wished him well. I hoped that he would soon find someone to keep him warm out there in the mountains, or at least a kinder and gentler brand of pornography.

—◻︎—

I spent many a long night trying to puzzle out that fiasco in Kobe, not unlike William Hurt in prison at the end of *Body Heat*.

I suspected Motoko of setting the whole thing up to torment me for so recklessly spermifying her after the Christmas party. But there was more to it than that. Having boasted to her friends about her gaijin lover, she now had to produce a body. So there I was: hauled in for a cameo appearance. Regrettably, no live demonstration would be required.

We went out once again after that, remarkably. She took the initiative, as usual, dragging me back to that same disco inferno we had gone to when we had first met. Her reflected image shook its breasts at me in the universal sign for "This is what you'll not be getting any more."

—◻—

I had been used! Right and left. I had been used and cast aside, like a once-cherished t-shirt now demoted to toilet-polishing duty.

My God, how demeaning. How debasing. How greatly like how it must feel to be a woman much of the time. What could be worse than to be so callously used and then discarded?

> *Teaching Point 11: It is better to have been callously used and then discarded than never to have been used at all.*
> *Especially by a Japanese chick with huge tits.*

Is this a great country? Or what?

LESSON 4

Don't do anything

"Oh, Auntie Em, there's no place like home."

You work at home. To no one's amazement more than your own, you have become a "popular" teacher. The House has whipped up a full-time contract for you: two scoops of free room and board with the cutest little salary on top.

No bills, few expenses, no dependents. Your savings grow like a cactus feeding off its own internal water supply.

The Widow Wakamatsu literally goes through a wall for you: the Room of Death is combined with the adjacent room so that you now have as much space to yourself as four Japanese residents do. You are obliged to work all of twenty hours per week. Commuting time from bedroom to classroom is ten seconds. Fifteen in rush hour.

It's like traveling back to that first quarter in the freshman dorm when you took everything pass-fail and slept till noon every day, except that now you're paid for it, while on the downside no one has a beer bong.

In the words of Ted Nugent, you have life dicked.

—◘—

In the lounge some of the Senko Seal boys are tuned into the *Explosive Laughter Hour*, a cacophonous sketch show based on the Japanese comedic principle that a gag which is slightly humorous when spoken in a conversational tone will become ten times funnier when screamed at ten times the volume. The boys aren't really watching; they just want to get away from their senior, Mr. Kaneda, who is already in his cups.

Mr. Kaneda is red enough to lead an ambush on the cavalry, but otherwise in no condition to do so. Instead, as is his wont, he dispenses kitchen-table advice to the lovelorn. He assumes (not without reason) that everyone around him is lovelorn.

A few other company men sit at the table, near enough to hear Mr. Kaneda and yet adeptly not hearing him. They came home too late for class and are now consuming the Saran-wrapped dinners that the House cook Mrs. Nakata left behind.

Among them is young Mr. Imazato, one of several residents who suffer from Negrophrenia, the unaccountable belief that they are not Japanese "salarymen" at all but rather downtown funkalicious seventies pimps.

Mr. Imazato greets a Housemate with a hearty "Hey, my niggah!" and from there they both know their lines by heart:

"Who you callin' *niggah*, niggah?"

"Heeeyyy, whaddit *izz*!"

"And whaddit *shall be*, bro!"

"This be *sho* good eatin'."

—◻—

"We want to learn black urban English," they told me.

I pointed out that I was not black, nor urban, nor had I ever been. They could check my résumé on file in the office if they doubted it.

"Just a few phrases. You're the only one we can ask!"

And I couldn't say no. After all, who's the cat that won't cop out when there's sociolinguistic ignorance all about?

Josh!

Right on…

And so it came to be that residents who could not express such concepts as "The dog is barking" or "I'd like lemon in my tea, please" were now fluent in some sort of abominable pimp-and-minstrel Creole of my own devising.

"Lezz go downtown, get us some *play*."

"You the *man!*"

—¤—

In the mornings, I taught a class in the House called, in a forehead-slapping paroxysm of naming genius, the Morning Course. It was not a rule that only chicks just out of high school could enroll, but this was generally the case.

The textbooks we used featured repetitive drills, and thus my mind was freed up for the ongoing project of imagining precisely what all my students looked like naked.

After Morning Course finished, I would have lunch with the girls and imagine what they looked like naked eating lunch.

Afternoons were for masturbation and siesta.

Then, I taught the evening class.

Its members worked or went to nearby colleges during the day and attended class weeknights from six thirty to eight thirty, if they were able and willing. A typical class held eight to ten souls, sitting in a horseshoe.

I handled the beginners' class. Its members were apt to be younger than I and thus both more pleasing to imagine naked and less likely to recognize me as the fraud that I was.

—¤—

"'You went to the concert.' Okay, Rumiko!"

"You went to the concert, *didn't you?*"

"Good! 'We're having chicken for dinner.' Natsuko!"

"We—we're having chicken for dinner…*aren't we?*"

"Yes! Okay, Doshita: 'I've given you my phone number.'"
"Y… Y… You—"
"No, listen: 'I've *given* you…my phone *number*.'"
"Y… Y… You—"
"*You're not listening!*"

Young Master Doshita was certainly a vexing pupil. While trying to respond, he invariably rocked from side to side and grimaced, churning his stubby, well-marbled arms as if trying to wrestle the English language into submission.

He deserved an antagonist every bit as inept in teaching a language as he was in learning one, and that's just what he got in Mr. Angelos. It was the classic case of the irresistible asshole meeting the immovable blockhead.

"I…I gived you my—"
"'I've *given* you'!"

Mr. Angelos's presence in the House, it must be said, added an essential dose of authority. We had been having a little too much fun for our own goods until he showed up to set some limits, sort of like the pilot at the end of *Lord of the Flies*.

Roelof and Fat Matt had been evicted after coming to blows over a chick named Tamiko, Matt's ex and Roelof's new girlfriend and far too fine a lady for either of them.[*]

Mr. Angelos, in his late thirties, with his ramrod posture and owlish glasses, scared us straight.

"I've-given-you-my-phone-number…"
"Yes?"
"…"

Japan's public broadcasting station began running BBC Shakespeare productions every Sunday night. Mr. Angelos recorded all of them. He midwived my fascination with

---

[*] In some weird but welcome bid to bat for the cycle, Tamiko knocked on my door too a few nights before her own inevitable departure to administer a clinical but vigorous guerilla handjob. She was fondly remembered by all whose lives she had touched.

HOW TO PICK UP JAPANESE CHICKS

Shakespeare as well as my lifelong penchant for pretentiously quoting him.

"Well?"

"I've-given-you-my-phone-number…*given't I?*"

"*Goddam it!*"

Mr. Angelos identified with the melancholy Jacques.

—◻︎—

But for summer intensive season when short-timers had to be added, our faculty consisted of Mr. Angelos, a wry red-haired Yalie named Eileen who became the bemused object of Mr. Kaneda's ardor, and me. Since we shared classes, we recorded each lesson's progress in a notebook for reference.

Monday, 10th. *Finished Unit 5; Exercise 3 (past tense drill) should be repeated. Everyone here on time for once, which was nice.*
Eileen

Tuesday, 11th. *Finished Unit 6, Exercise 1. Doshita stuttered through whole lesson. Resisted urge to shove blackboard eraser down his throat— barely.*
Angelos

Wednesday, 12th. *Finished Unit 6, all exercises. Should review Ex. 6. Ms. Kuga looking fine front and center. Used this notebook to conceal erection.*
Josh

—◻︎—

The warped and eroded exterior of the House was no match for the January winds. I came down with a nuclear flu.

Eileen brought me a card that she had induced everyone to sign. Others brought a Cadbury assortment of pharmaceuticals. A child of the seventies, I decided to wolf them all at once and see what happened. What happened was a searing of my throat by some vile granulated substance. It was like swallowing a pinch of Waikiki beach.

The first Japanese proverb that any male gaijin learns is *Sakè wa hyakuyaku no chô*: "Alcohol is the best of a hundred medicines." I was now in an excellent position to find out if alcohol was the best of at least twelve. I ventured to the far side of the house to raid the beer fridge.

On the way up the stairs, a tall chick galloped past me. I had not seen her before. Unbathed, unshaven, I must have appeared to be emerging from nine days in The Hole for spitting in the warden's coffee, but this did not dim her smile a single watt.

Maybe alcohol wasn't the best remedy after all.

— ◻ —

I knocked on the door.

"It's me. Want to go jogging?"

"Sure!"

It was two in the morning.

We covered variations of the same basic triangle on these midnight runs: Down the hill toward Maezono Park, along the tracks to Maezono Station, and then a killer sprint up the deserted hill.

She was not like other Japanese chicks. She ran in long, loping strides. She spoke English well—was placed in the intermediate night class—but "dainty" was not in her vocabulary.

When she laughed, she did not titter behind a palm. If a soprano can be said to roar, she roared. She gave you a full dental display and a *"Ha! Ha! Ha!"* She did this only when something actually struck her funny. She had great teeth. Nice cheekbones and shiny eyes, too.

There was no conscious effort at femininity about her. That's why I was so surprised one night when, in the midst of our panting, sweaty warm-down stretches at the end of the run, I kissed her under the trellis.

I was even more surprised that she let me: indeed, she seemed to expect it.

And I was more surprised still that I had the restraint to stop there and not ruin it.

Miss Hirano was just full of surprises.

—◻—

"Mr. Kaneda really likes Eileen," she said.

"I know."

"Eileen is really going to leave?"

"For a while. She's going to Thailand. She wants to help the refugees who come over from Cambodia."

"You must be sorry."

"Mr. Kaneda must be sorry."

"Is Eileen your girlfriend?"

"No. She's really just a friend."

"I hear you have a Japanese girlfriend."

"I did, kind of. But I haven't seen her for a few weeks."

It was in fact a few months since I'd seen the last of Motoko. Since then only Tamiko's drive-by handjob had broken the monotony.

"That's too bad."

"What about you?"

"Me? I don't have any boyfriend."

"You don't go out with people at the travel agency?"

"No. They are all old guys. Well, there's one young guy, but he reads dirty comic books all day."

"What about here in the House? You're very friendly with Mr. Wada."

"Wada-kun? *Ha! Ha! Ha!*"

So much for the Wada issue.

Without much effort on my part to lead it along, the conversation was going in a positive direction. And there we were, warming down out front of the House again at two thirty a.m. Would this be the night?

"What kind of girl," she asked, "do you like?"

"Hmm…"

A chick will try to measure your depth, or lack of same, with such a question by seeing whether you come up with a comment on character or appearance. Even as I saw the trap, I couldn't help stepping into it.

"In the House," she said. "For example, who do you like in the House?"

"Well, remember Miss Kuga? I think she left just after you came." A clever ploy, I thought, choosing a departed and therefore non-threatening rival.

"Kuga-san?"

"Um, yeah."

"You liked *Kuga-san?*"

"Um, kind of."

"Oh, no…"

No, this was not the night.

—◻—

As anyone who came into his gravitational field had heard time and again, Mr. Kaneda was the Senko Seal sales wizard who had secured Japan's number two domestic whiskey producer, Nikka, as a client for the company's bottle caps. Mr. Kaneda had ever since devoted himself to making Nikka number one.

Nikka stock was soaring on the eve of Eileen's departure for Thailand. Eileen made me stay up all night with her in the lounge. She was worried that Mr. Kaneda would snap out of his stupor and do something that might stain what she had already come to cherish as the memory of the most absurd courtship of her life.

"You figure to be there three months? Six?"

"Something like that. Depends on how long the refugee crisis goes on. And how long they let me stay."

"What'll you do after that?"

"Maybe I'll come back here for a while, maybe I'll go back home. Look for a job in New York. Something in publishing."

Mr. Kaneda stirred at the kitchen table. His movements were creaky and pained, like those of a cigar store Indian that had been brought to life and was sorely displeased about it.

"So, what's going on with you and 'Miss Hirano'?"

Eileen delighted in my insistence on formal titles.

"We go jogging in the middle of the night."

"And that's all?"

"We went to a movie in Kyoto once. But she invited Imazato to come with us."

"Oh, that pseudo-Negro?"

"And," I confessed, "I've invited her to my room a couple of times."

"How did that go?"

"She said she'd think about it."

"And?"

"I guess she's still thinking."

Mr. Kaneda went back under.

"Well, I really like her. She's cool."

I nodded.

"You ever see the way she talks to little kids in the neighborhood?"

I nodded again.

"She's a real human being, that one. Don't let her get away."

Around two o'clock, Miss Hirano came down and sat by me on the lounge sofa. We tried not to make her laugh for fear of rousing Mr. Kaneda.

Around four, she put her head on my shoulder and went to sleep.

—◻—

Ennui set in after Eileen's departure, the only good effect of which was the rare chance it afforded to use *ennui* in sentences.

"That goddam Doshita," said Mr. Angelos, launching a daily rant. In time it became hard to remember that Mr. Doshita's given name was in fact Masayoshi.

Much to Mr. Angelos's dismay, the more common title became "Night Manager Doshita" after the Widow Wakamatsu offered him a live-in staff position. Mr. Angelos had been counting the days until Mr. Doshita's term as a student expired and he would return to his remote hometown in Kyushu. But all that counting had been in vain.

Kyushu natives are known for their Latin-like temperament, and Mr. Doshita was no exception. His frustration at his inability to lay hands on his slipperiest foe—the English language—boiled over into other aspects of life, as was seen in the locally famed kitchen-knife-wielding incident that drove an American resident from the House. (Yet another in a long series of ugly chick-centric disputes.[*])

The refugee had been in charge of the House beer concession, a service far more valuable than any that Mr. Doshita would ever perform, and which I then assumed. I was responsible for ordering cases, keeping the refrigerator stocked, and collecting payment for bottles consumed at the end of each month.

---

[*] By which I mean that the disputes were ugly, not necessarily the chicks.

I ran superfluous promotional campaigns. That spring, there was the "catch the first cockroach of the year" give-away. But greater suspense was generated by the closest-to pool for guessing the exact date on which Obasan, our cackling and toothless cleaning woman, would stop greeting us in the morning with *Samui desu ne* (Cold today, isn't it?) and switch over to *Atsui desu ne* (Hot today, isn't it?).

By popular demand, I had to run that one in reverse the following fall.

—◻—

One night, jogging was rained out.

There was a knock on my door around one-thirty. Miss Hirano's pillow entered, followed by her.

"I'm going to sleep here," she announced. "Okay?"

"Okay."

She settled in under the blankets with her back to me.

"But *don't do anything*."

"Okay."

I ventured a hand over her shoulder, which she captured in her own hand.

"Did your roommates notice you leaving?"

"No roommates."

"What about Natsuko and the other two?"

"They all went somewhere."

That made sense. Two of her three roommates had hooked up with a couple of the younger Senko Seal boys. The other one just liked to sleep around. It didn't feel like that much of a triumph. I was simply bathing in the fallout of others' successes.

As per instructions, I didn't do anything. I even managed to fall asleep for a few hours, which made not doing anything easier.

> *Teaching Point 12: Don't do anything.*
> *All this jangling around creates friction in the atmosphere, which contributes to the melting of the polar ice. Unless you want that on your conscience, just stand still. Japanese chicks will come around. If not, you're beyond help.*

—◻—

Not doing anything paid dividends.

She came over regularly; she made fewer conditions.

We went around the bases in the traditional order—a good example of a cliché that never gets old. Especially third base, the old Hot Corner.

She apologized for having small breasts.

I could not say that they weren't small, but could honestly say that it didn't matter.

I did not say "I love you."

—◻—

Many American military campaigns are remembered for stirring slogans like *Remember the Alamo!*, *Remember the Maine!*

My battle cry was *Remember Lake Biwa!*

It was pretty timid as far as battle cries go, but timidity served me well.

Finally she said, "I would throw away my virginity for you."

I did nothing that night due to paralysis.

This was new territory for me, this chick clobbering me with her natural vulnerability. It was disarming. It was threatening.

It's an insidious biochemical agent in the Japanese chick arsenal for which Western Man has no defenses. I was as doomed as an Arawak tribesman who had been sneezed on by Columbus.

—◻—

A few hours of sleep. The dawn light crept in, diluted to a pale orange by the opaque window.

Our first time together was short. But there was nothing brutish or nasty about it.

LESSON 5

The cistern of your lust

*"But there's no bottom, none, in my voluptuousness.
Your wives, your daughters, your matrons, and your maids,
could not fill up the cistern of my lust."
"We have willing dames enough. There cannot be that
vulture in you to devour so many as will to greatness dedicate
themselves, finding it so inclined."*

—*Macbeth*

*We ought to just change the name to "International House
of Sex." Then maybe people would sneak around at night to
study English.*

—Mr. Angelos

In advance of the summer intensive course season, the office staff was upgraded with the addition of a Ms. Shimoda as day manager.

She was in her mid-twenties, fluent in English, sternly professional, proudly feminist, and recently liberated from the Island of the Amazons. Many a Japanese woman had by this time looked down on me, but she was the first to do so literally.

She was also the only Japanese woman I ever knew who worked in formal office-wear sans bra. It happened to be the first thing I noticed about her when, hung over, I went downstairs to introduce myself. Opening the sticky office door forced her to exert much upper-body torque, and I was as mesmerized as a cat eyeing a metronome. It was an awkward start to a lovely friendship.

—¤—

"Josh-sensei, Miss Endo wants to say something to you."

"Oh, hi," I say. "You guys are leaving today?"

"Yes!"

I am speaking to the generic "vivacious but unappealing chick who inevitably bonds with a heartbreakingly gorgeous chick." Miss Endo herself, the latter, tasers me with her wide brown eyes.

It is Sunday morning. It is time for one summer intensive course group to move out so that the next can move in. It is not uncommon for intensive course chicks to make the rounds of teachers' rooms for a few halting sentences about how moving, how life-course-altering—yea, how ineffably transcendental—the experience of meeting a real-live foreigner has been.

"Miss Endo likes you very much!"

"Is that right?" I ask Miss Endo's rep.

"Yes!"

"Ah. Well, then..."

"Miss Endo would like you to kiss her goodbye."

"Oh really?"

"Yes!"

"Would you excuse us?" I ask the rep.

Miss Endo and I stand alone in the hallway. She has pixie hair. She is slim, lithe, fawn-like in her slow blinking gaze. She is seventeen.

I know that the rep is peeping around the corner. That doesn't concern me. I fear the madman Mr. Doshita...with the knife, in the hallway.

I opt for hands on shoulders, lips on lips, no tongues. Five seconds at most. Well, what the hell—ten.

Ten, I said! Have to stop now, or there's no turning back...

—◻—

Intensive course season. It was certainly more fun the second time around.

Every week a new chick tsunami. Every week, the same chick-pleasing comedic material, the same chick shtick. If it's Tuesday, it must be time for the intentional pratfall in the direction of a gaggle of giggly high school chicks. If it's Thursday, why not break out the fake-electrocution-while-plugging-in-the-tape-player bit. It's C Group, the lowest level, so you go with your physical stuff. They eat it up.

On Wednesday afternoon, there's a tea party. You muddle through with heisted riddles and parlor games. Charmed chicks chuckle! Cheeriness achieved!

Saturday night, it's time for barbecue out in the field. After dark, when the bugs get bad, you all move to the lounge for the dance party. It used to be R&B, but this year it's disco. Mr. Doshita loves disco, especially Abba, and this is not a democracy.

Mr. Doshita has invested his entire salary in an array of ruffled shirts and suits so shiny that he might have skinned them from actual sharks. Early in the evening, he will clear the floor and turn up the lights for his solo number.

"That goddam Doshita," Mr. Angelos mutters. "I'm sorry they have such good gun control laws here sometimes."

Not for the first time, you look upon your senior colleague with concern.

Mr. Doshita's going for the Travolta thing, that much is clear: the sweeping arm arcs, the sudden spasms of footwork, etc. But he's too high-strung, too caffeinated. He wants to pull off the smoldering gaze, but he's obviously terrified. He invariably appears to be locked into one of those nightmares where no matter how frantically he tries to outrun the scrotum-chewing hell-hounds, his feet find no traction.

Mr. Doshita's number finally ends to polite applause. Another twenty-odd chicks are added to the expanding role of the Doshita Nonfan Club. Mr. Doshita sets the gold standard for not getting trim. On chicks' tricorders, he doesn't even register as a carbon-based life form.

The dance floor is reopened. You dance with chick after chick. You don't need to ask; they're just *there*, one after the other. There are jailbait chicks. There are married chicks ditching inert husbands for a week. And there are plenty in between: young, single, legal chicks. Fat chicks. Skinny chicks. Chicks who climb on rocks. Tough chicks, sissy chicks. Yes, even chicks with chickenpox. You revel in your God-given Caucasianness.

Then Sunday is transition day. Notebooks are thrust forward that you may inscribe your parting words of wisdom. Your hungover stare is captured in a hundred camera flashes. Your hands shake, but you shake hands. Maybe you kiss.

And then it starts all over again.

Yes, intensive course season was great the second time around.

It sure played hob with a relationship, though.

—◻—

"Oh, there you are."
"I'm not going to stay all night."
"Oh, you always say that."
"I'll go back before the other girls wake up."
"What's the matter?"
"Nothing."
"You okay? Really?"
"*Nothing.*"
"Want to go up the hill for a swim?"
"No."

Miss Hirano settles down next to me on the futon. The nights of doing Nothing are behind us. We do Everything now, though sometimes in a perfunctory manner.

"Did you have a nice time with the intensive course girls today?"
"Yes, I did."
"You like them?"
"I do. But I'm not going to have sex with them."
"Do you have to spend so much time with them?"

"I'm a House contract teacher now."

"I'm getting tired of this House."

"It's just intensive course season," I say, sounding like we've been living here all our lives.

"I don't know why you had to sign that contract."

"It's a good deal. I can save money."

"I'm thinking about moving to an apartment."

"How come?"

"It's expensive here. I need to save money too."

"Far away?"

"I don't know."

A long silence in the dark, as the embers of Everything cool and die.

"I really thought we could live together," she says, "until you signed that fucking contract."

She's getting good at swearing.

"You've actually thought about that?"

"I really love you."

I kiss her, hoping it will substitute for a verbal response.

—◻—

Farther up the hill is an elementary school with a 10-meter pool. It was Fat Matt who first discovered the place and taught us how easily its chain-link fence was overleaped.

Miss Hirano and I go up there often during the summer for midnight swims. You have to duck underwater when a car goes past because (said Fat Matt, conducting orientation) who knows, it might be the pigs, man.

We go out to movies and dinner in Osaka.

I buy an electric keyboard and serenade her with W.C. Handy blues tunes and early Bob Dylan ballads.

We hang out in my room a lot and play games: Scrabble (for which she gets a handicap), Uno and Battleship. One inspired night, I invent Strip Battleship.

We practice swearing.

I finally get to see what the inside of a love hotel looks like. A locally famous one is two train stops away. You enter, bend down to a knee-high window, talk discreetly with one of two dwarfish, kindly old ladies who take your money and whisper something that might as well be "Happy coitus!" and you're on your way.

Miss Hirano likes the love hotel. There is privacy. A girl can make noise here. When she needs to use the bathroom, she doesn't have to skulk around and risk bumping into fellow midnight skulkers. There is a bed that is wider than our House driveway and much more comfortable to lie on. There is a TV, and no legion of lounge lizards to fight over the remote with.

I like the hotel, too. But it is expensive. I am constantly amortizing the room charge in my head, calculating the yen-to-orgasms ratio.

In the morning, we go to a Denny's across the street that offers a good pancake set.

It becomes a tradition: Cram half a month's sex into one night, then carb up on pancakes. The scent of maple syrup still arouses me to this day.

I say *I love you* at last. I start saying it often. I like the way I sound saying it. I especially like the results it brings.

— ◻ —

Was it love?

Could be. I had no point of reference. Somehow I had expected more. What I felt above all was great relief at not having to worry about where my next orgasm would come from—or go.

Intensive course chicks were tempting, no question. As my relationship with Miss Hirano entered the plateau stage, I found that she was becoming the recipient of more and more lust that was authored by others.

The spermification volume for a single lesson of a single intensive course group was a thing to be reckoned with, as the table below makes clear.

Assumptions:
1. The ejaculate of a healthy average man contains 400,000,000 sperm cells.
2. I am, in this sense, a healthy average man.

Class members	Spermification estimate per two-hour lesson
Full-figured college chick	209,000,000
Full-figured college chick's not bad roommate	128,000,000
Some guy	0
Hot jailbait	172,000,000
Another guy	37,000,000
Naïve jailbait	141,000,000
Horny, well-preserved housewife	148,000,000
Ice queen	159,000,000
Total	**994,000,000**

$$994{,}000{,}000 / 400{,}000{,}000 = 2.485$$

In short, the sperm volume generated by a single two-hour intensive class totaled nearly two-and-a-half times capacity. That's a god-awful lot of excess sperm—and I might meet *three* comparable sperm-generating groups per day.

Like a survivor of Pickett's Charge returning to Gettysburg in old age, I look back on those days and marvel that I got through it—girlfriend or no. I was a walking, talking, ticking sperm bomb.

The prostate reels.

—◻—

"When she asks, *Why do the birds go on singing?* and *Why do the stars glow above?*, see, she's wondering why the world just goes on like usual. Because she's, you know, really, really *sad* that she just lost her lover."

Passing along a corridor one day, I overhear a class in which a temp teacher incorporates a pop standard into a lesson plan.

"And...and the part where she sings *Why does my heart go on beating?* and *Why do these eyes of mine cry?*... Well, that also means that she's, like, really, *really* sad."

I don't know what his class is thinking. Myself, I am wondering if I could ever feel like that. If Miss Hirano and I separate—*when* we separate, for it is inevitable—am I fated to go on some loopy tirade against the birds and the stars and sundry body parts just for going about their respective business?

No matter how meticulously a fellow educator might deconstruct it for me, I cannot grasp the essence of this song. Nor that of any other song dealing with Love—requited, unrequited, found, lost, whipped, pureed, or slathered with sauce and cooked over a low wood-chip flame till the meat practically falls off the bones.

In nineteen-eighty, tender love songs are just radio clutter between Blondie tunes to me.

—◻—

Chillin' in the office with my home-girl, Ms. Shimoda.

"How are your private lessons with Mrs. Wakamatsu?"

"Seriously? She's a total moron."

"Yes, but how are the lessons?"

"I don't think she's learning anything, and I don't know what to do about it."

"Well, she likes you."

"Widow Wakamatsu is one hot babe."

"I don't mean it like that. She thinks you're a good teacher."

"Oh."

"Does everything have to be…like *that* between you and Japanese women?"

"Do I have to answer that?"

"You're not going to… Well, you know what happened to Arthur."

"Don't worry. I've settled down. You know that I'm with Miss Hirano now, right?"

"I don't want to hear about it! I don't want to know what goes on in this House at night!"

She does a hear-no-evil pose and shakes her head, causing residual tremors in other areas. I'm chubbing.

"What's your purpose in working here," I say, "if you can't enjoy all the gossip?"

"I can use English here," she says. "I want to go to graduate school in the States someday."

"And study what?"

"TESOL."

"Huh?"

"Teaching English to Speakers of Other Languages. What *you* do."

"They actually give *degrees* in this hogwash?"

"I hope to be an English professor someday. I want to teach in a university."

"Good lord. Why would anyone want to *do* that?"

"*Samui desu ne!*" the cleaning lady finally screeches.

Fall falls on cue, and is glorious. Intensive season is over. It's just us now. Just the family.

"Are you coming to my room tonight?" I ask.

"It depends on Mrs. Wakamatsu," she replies.

The Widow has decided that she needs a better grasp of this business that she has inherited. During the slow season in fall, she takes to staying over. She has asked Miss Hirano if she could take the upper bunk, just for a night or two. Like a vampire, once invited in she cannot be driven out.

When she stays, Miss Hirano can neither sneak out nor sleep. The Widow Wakamatsu pours out stories of her horrid marriage to the late Mr. Wakamatsu. The listing of his sins is an epic tale and not a very efficacious bedtime story.

—◻—

"Kanako-san and I will get an apartment," she announces one night when she has made a break for my room. "It's that building just at the bottom of the driveway, where Mrs. Nakata lives."

"Oh, that close? That'll be good."

"I won't come here and sleep with you then."

"Sure, sure."

"I really won't."

"Then I'll come to you."

"It's a one-room place."

"I've always liked Kanako."

"I want to think about the future."

I don't.

"I don't know what's going to happen," I say.

"Are you going to go back to America?"

"When my novel's finished, yes."

"When will that be?"

"I don't know. But I don't think I can make it through another intensive course season here."

"I see."

"I really don't know what the future will hold."

Icy silence.

"Are you going to join that puppet theater?" I ask, hating dead air.

"I'll try when I save enough money."

Puppetry is her dream. Japan's best known such group operates out of Osaka. To join, she will have to audition, then work as an unpaid apprentice for a year before going pro.

In the meantime, she keeps working for a travel agency that offers businessman's specials: sex tours to Thailand. Her only joy is hearing the discomfort in the clients' voices when they call to make inquiries—*Can I just tell the wife that it's a golfing holiday? Or is it customary to actually bring the clubs along?*—and get a female voice.

"I can't tell what will happen in the future," I say.

I hold her in the dark, in the silence, but we do not sleep.

Teaching Point 13: The Future

There is something called a "future." Stay with me here, lads; this road gets bumpy. It seems that time extends beyond *our next orgasm and/or meal. Who knew?*

I would tell you more about the "future" thing, but being male I am still struggling with it myself. I can tell you, though, that everybody has one—with the exception of white male vocal groups—and that the gap in abilities to conceptualize this "future" thing is what leads to 97.4 percent of all inter-gender squabbles.

—◻—

December.

It's chilly in the lounge, even with the new heater. The Energy Crisis and all that. I'm sitting on the sofa watching the six o'clock news. The aroma of Mrs. Nakata's cooking wafts in. It'll be pork cutlets tonight. And miso soup. And shredded cabbage with mayonnaise. Always shredded cabbage with mayonnaise.

Sugar trudges in, just back from college, flushed from the cold. Without a word, she curls up in the seat next to me, runs her arm through mine so that her left breast is resting on it, and plops her head down on my shoulder. Her cheek delights my neck like the cool underside of a pillow. The scent of her shampoo overwhelms the cooking.

Sugar has a boyfriend. I have never seen him. He is a non-resident, a boy from her college, a pimply Romeo who sneaks into the House late at night and tries to sneak out before dawn. Mr. Angelos, the earliest riser in the House, has bumped into him and by his sheer charisma caused the lad to shriek, reverse course, and clamber down the fire escape. To hear Mr. Angelos tell it, this happens every single morning.

Now Sugar's cuter roommate Jailbait enters.

She glides toward my vacant side and assumes a position the mirror image of Sugar's.

The unusual thing about this scene is its utter usualness.

Mrs. Nakata comes out to wipe the dining room table. She has the central casting form of a cook: thickset, with tiny eyes far apart like a rhino's. She has cooked for me about seven hundred times. Our communication is mostly nonverbal, a vocabulary of smiles.

She smiles on the sofa scene. In her eyes, it is a scene of international domestic bliss.

AL ATI NS ITE NDER O ROO

—◻︎—

It was an early eighties Garden of Eden.

I sensed it while it was going on, somehow grasping that those days were not of the type that would only *seem* like the good ol' days as dimly perceived through a decades-scanning telescope. No, they *were* the good ol' days even as they unfolded, one good ol' day at a time.

I only wish I could seize the spirit of it. I have the photos, journal entries, other artifacts. But in the end, the spirit remains as slippery as that pesky phantom dagger that keeps dogging poor Macbeth.

I would not have traded my lot for anyone's—no, not even to be heir to the throne of medieval Scotland with all the willing dames in the country at my disposal. Those chicks, after all, would be Scottish. And medieval, which doesn't speak well for their personal hygiene.

But was it the Garden of Eden? Or Lotus Land?

I should go. Back to the real world. Back to pursue my art…

… … … … … … … … … …

Okay, maybe not right now, not this minute, with two chicks nuzzling me. By all means, let this moment play out.

But soon. Soon…

LESSON 6

Know when to fold 'em

*My conscience hath a thousand several tongues,
And every tongue brings in a several tale,
And every tale condemns me for a villain.*

—*Richard III*

Miss Hirano knew from the start that I would be leaving when my novel was finished. And soon it was!

Four hundred fun-packed pages about a lad who curses his loving mother, alienates all would-be friends, abuses his wife, dies in a drunk-driving collision and descends to Hell where Satan torments him with video clips of his squandered life over and over for all eternity.

"It's solid writing," my faculty advisor had once said after perusing an early draft, "but I just can't seem to feel any sympathy for the main character."

Friends who test-read for me responded with either frosty silence or fury. I was undeterred.

"An insightful tour of human nature's murkiest corners." "The dark new star of American letters." I fell asleep at night counting dust-jacket blurbs crawl over a fence like Slinkies.

—◻—

"I just want to focus on my writing," I said in the moonlight. "I'll never know if I'm any good or not until I do."

"You can do it in Japan, can't you?"

"I can't work in this House. There are too many... distractions."

"How about living somewhere else? And teach at a university? Some of the teachers who come here at night are teachers at GU."

"Yeah, but they're *real* teachers."

"You said Angelos is going to teach at GU from April."

"Good point."

"And he'll live in an apartment. Why don't you get an apartment? Then I could come there. Or we could live together."

"I can't be a university teacher, okay?"

"Why not?"

"I'm not a real teacher. Real teachers are assholes. I'm not one."

She did not point out the numerous fallacies in this argument. She said nothing.

"I need to go back to my country. I want to be American again."

"I want to live in America, too!"

"Maybe you will someday."

Long silence. Her breathing grew heavy, which signified either sleep, or an effort to fight back tears. Forced to bet my summer bonus, I would have chosen the latter.

Finally: "I want to come visit you in America once every year, even when I get old."

—◻—

She was living in a tiny apartment at the bottom of the House driveway now with her friend Kanako.

When so inclined, she padded up the hill in pajamas and sandals and stayed over.

One night it occurred to me that I was receiving oral gratification from a young woman in pink pajamas with cute farm animals printed on them—and this didn't seem at all odd to me.

I sure had been in Japan a long time.

—◻—

There was an international phone call for me in the office. A college friend calling from Minnesota.

"Sorry you had to wait. I was still in bed."

"What time is it over there?"

"I guess it's 10:30."

"And you were in *bed?* Jesus!"

"I work mainly in the afternoons and evenings these days."

"Huh. Well, I hear you're coming back soon."

"That is the plan. Should be back in two months."

"You gettin' lipstick on your dipstick?"

"I have a girlfriend, yes."

"Jap?"

"Um, yeah."

"Huh… Did you get my letter?"

"About the bar? Yes, last week."

"Okay, here's the deal. Randy knows this guy over in Sleepy Eye who has a bar for sale. It's a nice place, everything works. We could get it for about twenty-five grand. Interested?"

"I don't know. I haven't had my coffee yet. Maybe."

"Think you could borrow half of it?"

"I've got about twelve thousand in the bank now."

"You saved that in two years, just teaching English?"

"One year, actually. It took a year to pay back loans."

"Plus you sleep *till noon* every day, and you're *getting laid?*"

"Yep."

"And you're *coming back??*"

Ohhh, shit…

—◻—

Shit, shit. Shit shit shit shit shit…

Was I doing the right thing? *Was* it time to go?

Look at the signs:

One morning a huge yellow claw reached up from nowhere and dug itself into our yard. Gaining purchase in the ground, it pulled a Yanmar shovel vertically up the stone wall and into the adjacent field, which, we were rudely reminded, was not really our yard after all.

Sacred ground where we had enjoyed so many barbecue parties and nights of star-gazing, where wild marijuana planted by our gaijin forebears could still be found growing, where Jane the free-spirit Brit chick used to sunbathe topless—was desecrated and chopped into six roped-off parcels.

Six!

"The Japanese will build on anything," Ms. Shimoda said.

On weekends the developer—if not an actual yakuza, he could certainly get TV work as one—brought young families to tour the yard. I would set my speakers in the windows and bombard them with tracks from *Aladdin Sane*.

The yakuza made a rare weekday appearance to lambaste Ms. Shimoda, presumably over the stereo, and she apologized through clenched teeth. Then he stalked off to show a plot of land to a couple.

I volunteered to strip naked, dangle by one arm from the trellis and pleasure myself while gibbering like a chimpanzee.

Ms. Shimoda said, "Go ahead."

—◻—

Signs, signs, everywhere the signs…

The gaijin madness had seized on Mr. Angelos now.

In April, the formal beginning of the Japanese school year, he had moved to an apartment down the train line and begun his new day job at a nearby university while still coming back to the House for night classes, after which he would stay until the last train, drinking heavily. By May, he had ended Mr. Kaneda's seventeen-month streak as leading patron of the House beer concession.

He suffered an injury that he refused to explain and had to walk with a wooden cane—a huge, knobby thing that looked as if he had pried it from the jaws of a grizzly. One night as he sipped his beer on the sofa, he began to poke an annoying intermediate class man in the shoulder with the weapon.

"Get out!" he said. "It's past your bedtime."

It seemed all in good fun, but Mr. Angelos persisted.

"Get out! *Ge-e-et o-w-w-w-w-w-t!*"

The pokes turned to blows about the ribs and shoulders. The student, first flustered and now horrified, fled.

Mr. Angelos laughed.

It was the first time anyone could remember hearing Mr. Angelos laugh. It was falsetto, incongruous.

It was insane.

—◻—

I sat down one day to count the foreigners I had known during a mere twenty-three months in country who had lost their minds. There were many.

Then I counted those who had stayed in Japan over six months without overt signs of lunacy. It was a very short list.

In my own final days I would lure groups of intensive course chicks up to the elementary school pool, just so I could see them in swimsuits. Better still for those who neglected to pack a swimsuit.

A college chick came along one night determined just to watch. I was equally determined to toss her into the water in order to see how transparent her street clothes would get. But she was too tough for me.

The next day, she was showing off the fingerprint-pattern bruises on her arm.

A newly arrived teacher, Kevin, not yet inured to our ways and customs, looked at the bruises and then at me with trepidation.

—◻—

A few nights later I awoke—or came to my senses; it was hard to tell—with said college chick lying on one side of me and her not-bad roommate on the other.

College Chick (her real name long forgotten) was justly proud of her wares and on this night not at all shy about letting them be displayed and sampled. But then the Conscience DA intervened, that bastard.

My conscience had not a thousand several tongues, but the one tongue it did have more than sufficed to kill a good time. I suppose most everyone outside the Washington beltway gets mired down in internal debates with their consciences, though mine tend to be more formal than most.

In those days my conscience took the form of the black-and-white DA from the original *Perry Mason* series. The actor who played him did scary anti-smoking PSAs before dying bitter and winless, but lived on in my soul, determined to even up his record.

And just how do you justify this behavior, Mr. Muggins?

Um… Sperm volume is at 2.485 times capacity, after all.

You are aware, aren't you, that your long-suffering girlfriend might appear at your door in her animal-print pajamas at any moment?

Under the circumstances, that is a chance worth taking—don't you think?

No, Mr. Muggins. I do not think it is a chance worth taking.

HOW TO PICK UP JAPANESE CHICKS

Oh, come on, please. It's a sleeping-with-two-chicks story in the making. Every man deserves a sleeping-with-two-chicks story before he dies.

Where did you read that?

Nowhere... But it must have been in the earlier drafts of the Bill of Rights, don't you think?

As usual, glib and irrelevant.

Look, doesn't this prove what I've been saying all along? That I'm not ready to commit to my girlfriend? That I need to go back to my country?

So you think you can risk inflicting the pain of this scene on your girlfriend just to prove that point? The prosecution rests. No, the prosecution simply throws up it hands. No, strike those last two words. The prosecution simply throws up.

Was he right? I don't know. But he won.

College Chick and roommate were sent home. Long-suffering girlfriend did not appear. I was left to dump the excess sperm the old-fashioned way, and to ponder the what-ifs.[*]

—◻—

---

[*] I did not have to ponder long. Newly arrived Kevin proved a quick learner. Channeling the spirit of Fat Matt, he seduced College Chick a few nights later and subjected us to an excruciatingly florid play-by-play the following morning.

Not a lot was said on the last night, nor needed to be. She sniffled a while, then slept. I sniffled a while, then contemplated the odds of getting College Chick and her roommate back over to celebrate my new singlehood once Miss Hirano had left for work.

These thoughts stirred the interior DA to action, but I shushed him.

In the morning, I watched from my window as she bounded down the driveway in that loping, boyish stride that had first drawn me to her. She couldn't see me through the tight mesh of the screen but turned to look anyway.

Two strides later, the mossy stone wall erased her from view. And then that wall, so it seemed, fell on me.

Ohhhhhh, shiiiiiiit.

Teaching Point 14: Don't look back.

No, I mean do *look back. I mean…oh hell, what are you listening to me for? If you haven't figured it out by now, there's no point in it, no point at all.*

Listen to me and I'll only knock your soul out of the smooth, taken for granted orbit that it's probably been wafting in for years, causing it to re-enter earth's atmosphere at an awkward angle whereupon it will incinerate and leave charred flakes across ten western states.

Oh, mothers, tell your children not to do what I have done…

My god, my god… I am so full of shit…

LESSON 7

The fear of God

Thou shouldst not have been old till thou hadst first been wise.

—*King Lear*

I yam what I yam.

—Popeye

1

Ayana breaks through the rush-hour throng at Yokohama Station much like a baby shark might thrash its way out of the womb.

Before her email inviting you out to dinner, you had never thought of her as a potential evening companion.

Such deference toward a young Japanese woman was not the result of any spiritual epiphany since your departure from the House some seventeen years earlier—although there had indeed been one. Nor was it an epiphany of common sense, though there should have been one of those by now, too: one would expect you to have heard Last Call for College Chicks at least a decade earlier, being as you turned forty a year ago.

It's just that the campus of the private university at which you and she met is so saturated in chicks who seem genetically engineered to produce Evening Companion fantasies that one of Ayana's middling caliber cannot be appreciated until she breaks free of the pack.

And could this be part of her plan?

Did she *have* a plan?

She's rambling on about various Californians who have come to your campus for the semester abroad exchange.

Ayana befriended a great many of them over the years, male and female alike, and so possesses an encyclopedic knowledge of their quirks and peccadilloes. She's the J. Edgar Hoover of the Department of International Relations.

"You know that girl Izumi? She was in one of your classes, right?"

"Uh-huh."

"Well, she had this big thing for that blond guy Storm."

Storm. Even the names make you feel old.

"But Storm didn't like her at all. And one day she comes up to me and goes, 'You'd better stay away from Storm. I saw him first!' To *me!* Can you *believe* that?"

"Um, no."

"As if I was hooked up with Storm!"

"You weren't?"

"Oh, God, no. He had a girlfriend back in San Diego."

"Ah."

"Then Storm got all paranoid because this Izumi was stalking him…"

This is all a bit more than you bargained for. One by one, seemingly normal, nondescript students from years gone by are unmasked as drooling psychopaths. You've always assumed your female students would be shocked to know what evil lurks in the heart of their English teacher. Now you find out it's a two-way street.

The dessert course a memory, you assume you are excused. Ayana says, "You wanna go to a bar?"

"I mean, as far as the school is concerned it's Rumiko this, Rumiko that."

Now she's savaging a former classmate no longer alive to defend herself. The Rumiko in question visited the Philippines for a month-long study trip, then upon her return to Japan promptly got killed in a traffic mishap. Her grieving parents provided an endowment that led to the foundation of an NGO, and the university has milked years of PR from the romantic tale.

"It was *us* who built up the organization. It was *us* who got the grade school in Zamboanga up and running."

"Uh-huh."

"Me and Kumi and Tomoka and Shintaro."

You're both seated in bolted-down, sadomasochistic bar chairs, knee to knee. You are bonding; at a molecular level, so are your antiperspirants.

"But do we get our pictures in the school brochure?"

"No, you don't."

"Damn right we don't!"

Her eyes are close together. Her lips are wide and thin. The type of man who looks for such flaws will find them and tabulate them. But you are over forty, barely clinging to your immortal soul, and not at all choosy.

"I mean, for God's sake," sputters Ayana, putting another tequila sunrise on your tab, "all the girl did was *die*."

—◻—

A few days later, you send her an email thanking her for the lovely evening and adding that oh, by the way, you sure would like to see her naked.

She responds with righteous indignation and a proposal to meet again on Saturday afternoon.

—◻—

"You know what really pisses me off?"

By this time the list includes the ludicrous registration error that delayed her graduation by a semester, her snooty coworkers at the trading company, her inept boss at same, the slowness of American grad schools to respond to application inquiries, you, Professor Asada's habit of rubbing girls' backs when he gets liquored up, guys she has liked who didn't return the feeling, English education at college apart from your classes, and lucky dead chicks who get all the credit.

"No. What pisses you off?"

"Sarcasm."

"Like what?"

"When I was in California last spring to visit friends, I was hanging out with this guy—"

You don't think the anxiety shows, but as usual you're a shallow read.

"Hey, nothing happened! Nothing ever happens to me with guys."

"Okay."

"Anyway, I'd say something like 'Let's drive by the beach,' and he goes, 'Oh yeah, we *really* want to do that in this traffic.'"

"Ah."

"And it was like that all the time! 'Oh, that's a *great* idea.' 'Oh, that's what I *live* for.' Why can't he just say, 'I don't want to do that'? What is it with you Americans and your sarcasm, anyway?"

"Um, I don't know."

"Anyway… I heard about this neat temple but it's way up top of the hill. You want to go look for it?"

"Oh, I *really* want to do that in this heat."

—◻—

The relationship pricked the interest of the Conscience DA right off.

Dating a student? At your age? Oh the shame. The shame.

Look, she graduated eight months ago. Anyway, she started it.

This is not a sandbox quarrel, Mr. Muggins. This is the soul of a naïve and innocent child!

She's twenty-three and knows what she wants.

Let the record show that when you *were twenty-three you were committing mass acts of sexual harassment in a tent at Lake Biwa.*

Point taken. But girls mature faster than boys, you know.

You are a very bad man, Mr. Muggins.

Oh dear, no. I'm a very good man. I'm just a very bad wizard.

—¤—

I certainly tried being a good man. It just didn't take.

A few years after I came back to Japan, master's degree in hand, to take my first real teaching position at D University, I started to exhibit symptoms of multiple sclerosis. I'm an MA with MS, *I thought.* What a résumé! *For once, I failed to amuse myself.*

There were tests, including one in which my head was immobilized while a round shower curtain with pasted-on pictures of bunnies and Santa Clauses whizzed about me. After a few minutes of this, I was expected to walk steadily. I failed.

The tests were ambiguous, but with a long family history of various nervous system disorders, I was sure of the verdict.

When the word came back that I was cleared, the remaining symptoms—but for a residual aversion to Santa—vanished.

I switched my allegiance to the other Christmas icon.

—◻—

The plan for Saturday's outing is a tour of some of the many shrines and temples of Kamakura, the ancient capital just to the south of Yokohama.

You meet at North Kamakura Station and have lunch at a little Mexican place nearby. It's famous among foreigners, Ayana says. Why, she has often seen Mr. Furman, your superior in N University's English program, eating here. You wolf down the rest of your burrito.

You embark up a narrow trail into the rolling wooded hills. The sun is brutal during the unshaded stretches; Ayana's effortless stride in front of you chides you for your lack of exercise. Or is it just age?

As if in response, a stiffy rises defiantly in your jeans as you eye the constant swaying of Ayana's buttocks, now at eye level on the steep path. *She will bear you many sturdy sons*, intones a weird interior voice.

Each of the several shrines along the path envelopes you in a cool, cedar-scented oasis of perfect calm. You purify your hands with water from the sacred troughs. You sit on mossy rocks and catch your breath.

Some of these shrines are so small and off the tourist track that they are completely deserted. Not so much as a booth selling *omikuji* fortunes to be found. There are wooden chests, through the slats of which one can drop a monetary contribution—or not, if one's spiritual needs are not sated by the shrine's ambience.

HOW TO PICK UP JAPANESE CHICKS

Wherever you go—Buddhist temple or Shinto shrine—you splinter the spiritual calm by bitching about your jobs.

"Do you know what I'd like to do to Mr. Furman?" you ask, seated on the stone steps of an ancient temple's main hall.

"What?"

"You know those blow-darts that Amazon Indians use? I'd like to shoot him with one of those. Then I'd lay him flat on the ground, paralyzed yet still fully conscious. And then I'd squat over him and shit into his open mouth."

"Oh, *that's* a nice thought to share just after lunch."

"Hey! Sarcasm!"

—¤—

Then you arrive at a temple so breathtaking in its sylvan purity that even you shut up.

You have climbed a steep stone staircase to the top of the world. You are in a thick bamboo forest. You follow other pilgrims through it on a path of raised stones. The height of these stones and the gaps between them make the walk an act of concentration not unlike the final stage of an Indiana Jones quest. A wrong step here might not release some medieval decapitation device, but a sprained ankle is a possibility.

It doesn't matter much because no one on this single-file trek, yourselves included, is in any hurry for the path to end. On both sides are endless tableaux of bamboo: leafy green sprouts, their utility-pole-thick grandparents, and everything in between—all reaching in parallel perfection up to the sky and beyond. The random splays and splashes of light that seep through take on an unearthly emerald hue, as if born of some much more enchanting source that our dreary old sun.

The chorale of the cicadas crescendos and diminishes and crescendos again. The scent of greenness itself floods the bloodstream like a chlorophyll fix.

No one says a word.

—◻—

Merely joining a church was not enough. The karmic debt was too great. I became one of the organists, taking a monthly turn in the rotation.

As it was an all-Japanese church I could understand only half of the sermons, yet I alone among the flock kept eyes open for the full fifty minutes of abstract Biblical deconstruction.

To make up for my failure to grasp nuances at church, I undertook to read the whole Bible from cover to cover at home. I did skim over the Old Testament guidelines on chucking out furniture that a menstruating family member might inadvertently have sat on—drunk as I was on the Holy Spirit, this just seemed wasteful as well as irrelevant—and likewise skipped any compendium of begats.

The rest I read in earnest. And wrote about, as well, in shocking and unwelcome letters about "the Word" to old friends back in the Great Satan.

—◻—

"My boss tries to speak English in the office."

"It's nice that he tries."

"No, it's annoying. He translates everything literally."

"Like what?"

"You know the expression *atama ni kuru*? It's sort of like 'pissed off.'"

"I know it now."

"Can you guess how he translates that?"

"'It comes to my head'?"

"Exactly! *Why doesn't anybody answer that phone! It comes to my head!*"

"How old is this guy?"

"I don't know but he's ancient. At least forty-two."

"That's just plain mean…"

"Want to go to the beach?"

You have arrived at the end of the trail, the main Kamakura Station.

"To swim?"

"No. It's just nice there."

—◻—

"Come on!" She slips out of her shoes and rolls up her jeans.

She's prancing in the surf! At sunset! And so are you!

Well, kind of. You were never much of a prancer, truth be told. If you were a reindeer, you'd be one of those back-of-the-pack boys, Donder or Blitzen.

Ayana, now writhing in place, was certainly trying out for Vixen.

You move in on her. For a moment, it seems you might be Dasher after all. She does this incongruous, coquettish oh-you-naughty-boy posture with her hands knitted behind her, her hips swaying as she slowly backs away from you.

And down in your pants, there arose such a clatter; it sprang from the Hanes and it kept getting fatter…

"Let's go have dinner."

"What? Okay. Where?"

"How about Fujisawa?"

—◻—

A funny thing happened on my way to beatification.

A sophomore girl from D University invited herself to my apartment.

She was eager to study abroad and wanted to go over some advanced study materials. Curiously, she neglected to bring those materials with her. Instead she brought pictures. Of herself.

My apartment then was a studio—little more than a replica of my old IHE Room of Death with a kitchenette and unit bath tacked on. My futon lay folded up in a corner for lack of storage space. My furnishings were a low table and zabuton *cushions on the floor.*

The only decorations were framed photos of my great-grandfather and two maiden great-aunts, all Episcopal missionaries who had devoted their lives to converting the heathen in Japan. They seemed to sense the creeping recrudescence of my impure thoughts, and they were not happy about it.

Yumiko came and saw and very nearly conquered. She was petite, freckled, poised and wily. She was clearly an agent of Satan.

She plopped herself down on the wadded-up futon as if it were a sofa, and bade me sit next to her. She plied me with pictures of herself in a swimsuit. In one, she was posed behind a fence so that its top and bottom rails neatly concealed her bikini.

"Why, it almost looks as if you're not wearing anything at all," I said, and then filled the dead air with a parched "ha, ha, ha."

"Do you have any pictures in a swimsuit?"

"If I did, I don't think you'd want to see them."

"Because you have a hairy body, you mean? Oh, don't worry about it. I like a hairy guy."

As I suspected: Satan's spawn sent to tempt me.

"At least I think I do. I've never known one. I like Sean Connery, though. Your beard makes you look like him."

"Oh, do you think so?"

"Take off your glasses."

—◻—

To you, Fujisawa is a station located in the province of Places South of Your Apartment that You've Heard of But Never Go To. It turns out to be a hot spot of clubs, game centers, and restaurants of all sorts. And Ayana knows the whole town, just like she knows the Yokohama Station area, and Kamakura, and for that matter most of Tokyo.

Does this chick do anything but explore and memorize cool nightspots and obscure scenic locales? Or have you just become that much of a recluse? You suspect the latter.

She takes you to an Italian place she knows, where you dine *al fresco*. Midway through the second bottle of wine, she tells you that she is a virgin and is mightily disgruntled about it.

She does not actually say, "I'm a virgin, and mightily disgruntled about it." There is code language involved. *I've never had a boyfriend... Only had a couple of real dates... Never really liked any guy that much... Couldn't talk to guys...*

You sit very close. Skin graft close.

"I mean, this one guy kept acting like he really liked me, and I liked him, too. I kept dropping these hints that I wanted to go out, but he never asked me. You ever have anything like that happen? Doesn't it just make you crazy?"

"It comes to my head."

You thus make wine come out her nose. You are proud of that.

You say, "Maybe we should walk around for a while."

This is code talk, too.

—▫—

I obliged re removing my glasses. I squinted into the eyes of the wicked sorceress. She sure didn't look evil. But I knew what would ensue if I weakened here.

The return of my symptoms. Tremors. Dizziness. Leprosy. (I still knew the word for that one.) The slow, miserable deaths of all my kin and chattel. A dozen years of drought. It was all in the Book.

"My goodness, you really **are** *shy, aren't you?" she said.*

And after some awkward small talk, she was gone.

I did it! I passed the test! My ancestors beamed down upon me: Well done, young Skywalker.

A few hours later, I curled up for the final reading of the day. It was Paul again, going on about circumcision...again. And on, and on... And then I snapped.

Who the hell cares whether or not the Galatians or Thessalonians or whoever trim their wicks? And who is Paul to hector them about it? He wasn't even an original apostle. He was a last-minute sub, like Ringo. Nothing against Ringo here, but why would anybody bring him in on an elective surgery issue?

Fish or cut foreskin—that's what I'd tell the Thessalonians. Do whatever makes you feel good about yourself, and to hell with what some johnnie-come-lately apostle or your glowering ancestors have to say.

Yes, for God's sake, do what feels good with your body once in a while. And with the bodies of adorable sophomore chicks who spend an hour and a half on trains—or donkeys, if you're stuck in the ancient world—to come up to your shitty little room to spread some joy around.

Never again, *I muttered aloud, invoking the motto of the City of Hiroshima to somewhat more trivial and selfish effect.*

Never again would I allow such an opportunity to walk out the door.

—◻—

You walk around with her, sure enough. Around and around. It seems after a while that you are as apt to stumble into Thessalonica as to find what you are looking for.

Ayana notes that the last train up to Tokyo, where she still lives with her parents, will be departing soon.

Surely this is the right part of town. Small seedy taverns and noisy game centers abound. There are side-streets that lead into side-side-streets, but none of them yield that precious lavender neon glow that you seek. Meanwhile, the last-train theme is oft reprised.

Finally you go for the one-handed buzzer-beater from half court.

"We're not going to find what I'm looking for," you say, pulling her aside. "So I wonder if you'd like to come back to my place tonight."

"*Your* place?"

The tone, the crinkling of the nose, and most especially the baring of upper teeth do not bode well.

"And do *what*?"

"That remains to be seen."

Even more intense nose crinkling and teeth baring.

"*Really*? Are you *serious*?"

"Then again, maybe some other time."

—◻—

Like Pistol at the end of Henry V, *I vowed to turn bawd after the debacle with Yumiko. Alas, in one's late thirties it's not that easy to turn bawd. If it were, everyone would do it. Far easier it proved to turn bald.*

Still, my move that year from predominantly male DU to predominantly female NU was an auspicious step. Every day I ascended to a hilltop Citadel of White where a DU chick like Yumiko would be lost amid the heav'nly host.

That NU was a Christian institution did not, in itself, impede my bawdy ambitions. Apart from a chapel in one corner of campus where I would occasionally deliver the lunch hour "message" and a creepy, hollow-eyed bust of our Yankee founder, there were no overt signs of our religious affiliation. Certainly there were no signs of it in the attitudes and behavior of our students. None at all in their summertime wardrobe selections, God bless their souls and belly-buttons.

I did not turn my back on God, but sought to negotiate some slack on the whole looking-upon-Japanese-chicks-with-lust issue. "You knew what You were doing when You created them so irresistible," I chided during an evening prayer, but in that awful moment God was silent.

Anyway, I found that bawdiness in a gracelessly aging English teacher was not a winning ticket. Godliness, on the other hand, proved unaccountably sexy. It was a Sisyphean catch-22 that was to be tested and retested over the years: Whenever troubles with my health drove me to fear for my immortal soul, I immediately attracted Jezebels intent on stealing that soul away. But once inspired to act on their seductions I suddenly acquired all the charm of a dysenteric wolverine.

If a better actor, I could have faked the Godliness. But no. The real thing—and Japanese chicks could sense it the way a shark smells blood—could only be produced by the Fear of God.

—▢—

Unsated I was, but not unloved. I soon found a home in the White Citadel on the Hill.

I was a taskmaster and a tough grader. I handed out surprise quizzes while the starting bell was still echoing. I piled on homework.

I wrote three albums of original songs and sold them at the autumn school festivals to raise money for MS research. I had a website with a "zine" featuring the must-read "Great Women of NU" interview series. Chicks vied for the honor of shaving my head.

I was a must-invite for parties, some of which (so I might be told at the last minute) were to be held at my home, a new and larger apartment within walking distance of campus.

I was called "Muggins." No first name. Not Mr. Muggins. Not Muggins-sensei. Not even Muggins-san. Just "Muggins" as in, "Hey, Muggins, we're coming over tonight. You gonna be there?"

I was a one-name artist. I was "that weird-looking teacher-like guy that you can actually talk to."

It was a cool position, good work if you can get it. But the whole shebang rested on my code of ethics: a house of cards built on sand.

Teaching Point 15: Be holy of heart and pure of mind. But check where your love hotels are located in all likely dating spots, just in case.

2

I'm not her first NU faculty member. Not even her first English teacher.

Over Vietnamese spring rolls, Ayana is telling me all about Samuel, a colleague who has since returned to his native Kenya. A two-meter black tower of rectitude in his lunch-hour mini-sermons at chapel, he was in fact no less fallible a human than I. "Actually, he was much worse than you," Ayana assures me.

Samuel used the old cultural exchange ploy. He lured her to his apartment on the pretext of giving him Japanese lessons for pay. Samuel was in fact prepared to pay a good deal more in exchange for a good deal more.

The Much Worse Than Me Club by now features an all-star cast including Professor Asada, the serial back-rubber—rumored to have gone much further with some chicks, and still active in the game well into his fifties—among others.

I wonder where I might fit into this litany once she finds the next man that she can talk to about such things.

—◻—

One night on a cross-town train, we are scanning the ads for English language schools, tour packages and the like and simultaneously lock onto one for a weekly scandal rag.

Oh look, there's a picture of kindly old Professor Harimoto from NU. Is he writing for those people? What an odd way to pad one's publication list…

Ayana has been reading ahead of me, and is stunned. Kindly old soon-to-be ex-Professor Harimoto is not a contributor; he's the catch of the day. The great man's wife is in the hospital recovering from a suicide attempt after discovering his long-time mistress.

—◇—

Freud asked, "What do chicks want?" I ask, "To heck with the rest of them. What does *Ayana* want?"

"The beers are on me," she says as we approach the bar at the blues club in the Ebisu district.

So it isn't the freebies. She often pays her share.

Is it free English practice? We speak Japanese half the time, too, so that isn't it.

And she has made plain that it isn't a physical attraction.

She wants just a friend? A buddy?

I ponder the crowd on the dance floor while I wait for the return of my—what? Girlfriend? Short-time companion? There is a mix of ages out there, but male gaijins and Japanese females dominate the demographics.

"Mr. Furman comes here quite a lot," she says.

"Jesus!"

"No, Furman."

I scan the floor all around for Mr. Furman, who is dwarfish and stealthy.

"Stop bringing me to places Mr. Furman comes to a lot!"

She sees that I am serious but laughs a mocking laugh.

Perhaps she views me as the "safe" male that can be confided in, the out-of-the-game chappie, like that coveted fashion accessory of women the world over, the One Gay Friend.

Okay, fine. In an attempt to neuter myself for our meetings, I take to preparing little worksheets of questions. Like a recovering alcoholic's AA poker chip, the paper can be plucked from a pocket to ward off the urge to flirt or seduce.

Despite my best efforts to bottle it up, however, my heterosexuality keeps on oozing through. But what the heck. If it's a buddy relationship she wants, she will have to put up with my kind of buddy topics.

"Let's see," I say, scanning a print-out. "Which member of your class would you say is most likely to get rich?"

"Rikako. She works at Takashimaya, in the men's wear department. She meets rich guys all the time."

"Being cute as a button doesn't hurt her chances, either. Which one is most likely to end up living in a cardboard box in the bowels of Shinjuku Station?"

"Well, I guess Masato. He never did find a job. We could go and look for him there tonight."

"Not tonight, thanks… Which member of your class would make the best stripper?"

"Hmm, that's a good one… Ah! I got it! *Yuri!* Yuri."

"Yes, Yuri would be good. I'd pay to see that."

"She's so brave. I bet she'd do it."

"Yes, she's great. Nice tits, too."

"Well, uh, they're so big."

"One day years ago at school, I was looking out the window on the top floor of Building 3. She saw me from the street and waved. I remember thinking, 'My God, they look huge even from five floors up.'"

"Damn her."

"You think they're visible from space?"

"I really wouldn't know."

"I would have picked Hanae, though, for the stripper."

"I don't like her, to tell the truth."

"*Fabulous* tits."

"I suppose so, but *I don't like her.*"

"Surprisingly mushy, though. I remember the day she passed the selection to study abroad, she ran up to thank me and hugged me hard. They just sort of…deflated. Like inner tubes shot with a nail gun."

"Why do you think I want to hear this?"

"A man never forgets a hug like that."

—◻—

Speaking of things a man never forgets, Mr. Muggins, shall we move on to the night of third July?

Oh, let's. God forbid we should leave that one out.

Did you or did you not maul Ayana's breasts without her consent?

You see, there's always a seed of truth in these things, and then so much fertilizer gets piled on.

You have heard the woman's testimony, sir, and you are under oath.

Yes, yes. I *gently cupped* one of them for a moment, and she was quite surprised.

Play with the wording all you like, Mr. Muggins, but is it not clear that you committed a blatant act of sexual harassment upon a former student, a young lady who admired you as a teacher, who looked to you for guidance, who placed the highest trust in you?

I admit it.

Do you not agree that your craven act merits swift and severe punishment?

Isn't humiliation in front of these dozens of readers enough?

—◻—

Cousin Avery (once removed) pops over to Japan for a five-day business trip, and is suddenly on the other end of a phone call to my room.

He wants to meet over the weekend. I say okay.

In my mind, Cousin Avery Once Removed is nothing more than one L-shaped chunk in the Tetris pile of pre-adolescent cousins-once-removed who would assemble for their annual three-day cage match at my aunt's house every Christmas. He has no independent identity.

All of a sudden, he is twenty-three, fresh out of college, employed by a major US manufacturer, and sounding ominously like a frat-boy.

Terrified, I send an SOS to Ayana.

"I'm sure he'd be enthralled by the exotic charms of a native girl like you."

"Yeah, yeah, yeah," she says, "I'll bail you out."

—¤—

Ayana takes us to an *okonomiyaki* restaurant. She looks better than ever in a white tank top. She has done something to her naturally kinky hair that makes it glimmer.

Avery is a cherubic clump of energy. This is his second trip to Japan, and he demonstrates his comfort level to us and our waiter by demanding "*Shibireru kudasai*" which, he is confident, will result in the delivery of three beers but instead means—if anything—"Please benumb me."

Ayana is starting to have fun in spite of herself under Avery's dogged interrogation:

How old are you? What do you do? Do you like it? Why don't you quit, then? What do people around here do on weekends? Well, what do you do then? Oh, there's a blues club near here? Live music and a dance floor? Really? Can we go?

When Ayana needs a respite, I drag Avery back to earth with thrombotic questions about the family back home, or what is popular in the States these days.

The latter tack brings forth a lengthy monologue about the recent movie *Swingers*. I think Avery will be gratified to know that I have seen and rather liked it too, but this is like telling an Islamic fundamentalist that Mecca seems like a cute and funky little town. Avery has committed large portions of dialogue to memory and is determined to teach them to both of us that we might better appreciate this enduring masterpiece of late twentieth century American cinema.

Family is the safer topic. I invoke the natural right of older relatives to bore youngsters with family history, specifically an introductory course on our common ancestor, my maternal grandfather.

Widowed in his fifties, I explain, he kept his machinist job in a local parts factory till the day he died at seventy-six.

"He never remarried?" Ayana asks.

"I think he was happy as a widower. He flirted with the ladies at the plant all day. And in the old family pictures with grandma, he always looked so small and timid. But in all the pictures we have after she died he's always lit up and having a great time."

"So," Ayana says, "this is your ultimate goal? You want to be widowed, alcoholic, and alone?"

—¤—

The club, thank God, is once again a Furman-free zone. Avery loves it at first sight. It looks like a place where the guys in *Swingers* would hang. It is *money*.

He wants to dance right away and, by process of elimination, his partner of choice is Ayana. Even with more choices available, he still might have gone with Ayana. He seems smitten.

He isn't the only one.

To defuse the dance issue momentarily, I give Avery funds to go get us drinks. Since the bar staff all speak English here, we needn't fear that he will return benumbed and beerless. Ayana and I wait near the restrooms, where a partition blunts the fury of the music and grants us privacy.

"What do you think of Avery?"

"He's really a nice guy! But don't leave me alone with him for too long, okay?"

The presence of our youthful sidekick has given our relationship a whole new dynamic. Suddenly, Ayana *needs* me. I am her protector. This knowledge infuses me with a new boldness that, mixed with the dinner drinks, nudges me off the Acapulco cliffs of common sense.

"You know, I'd really like to kiss you and touch your breasts right now."

"Uh-huh," she says, which, upon later reflection, meant, *Yes, I am aware of your desire to kiss me and touch them, and so what?*

"Is it…okay, then?"

"Uh…"

There is no signal of assent, but none of denial either. I move in, lips pursed, raising my left hand to trace a line along the underside of her right bra cup.

She recoils.

"Sorry! I thought—"

"God!"

"I mean, I thought—"

A two-beat pause, after which Avery returns with sitcom-like timing.

"Oh, here you are! Here's the brewskies! Can I set these here? Now come on! You promised me a dance!"

"I did?"

But resistance is futile. She is dragged onto the dance floor. I watch her go, see the plea for help in her eyes as the flailing crowd swallows her up, but do nothing. She is caught in the vortex of two heirs to the hormones of Poppa Ray Scofield, renowned blue-collar gigolo, and there is no escape.

—◻—

Avery's style is a nineties gloss on the timeless Aggressive White Man school of dance that I recognize from my college days. He pounds one foot into the floor, occasionally grabs Ayana by the hand and twirls her around, then welds his eyes shut and shakes his fists in a spasm of what, in my generation, was known as *getting down tonight*.

During one of Avery's self-absorbed blackouts, Ayana, now smiling the most plastic smile ever smiled in all the epochs since early hominids evolved the capacity for duplicitous smiling, waves for me to haul her back to shore.

As a principle I enter crowded dance floors with about as much joy as I might wade into a pool of battery acid. But here is a chance, I am thinking, to redeem myself.

I wedge myself in. I prod Avery out of his rapture.

"May I cut in?"

"Hey, Josh! It is *on*, baby. It is *so on*!"

—◻—

The only dance I know is the Antler Dance. I have hopes that this will amuse Ayana, or at least ease her mind in that my hands will remain safely atop my own head, fingers a-wiggle to simulate antlers.

But not so.

"Admit it," I say, insistently antler-dancing. "You're getting tired of my whole family."

She either doesn't hear me or she does. There is just the plastic smile and not very much eye contact.

"You're pissed off, aren't you."

Nothing.

"I guess we really 'came to your head,' huh?"

Even the old standards fall flat.

The music stops.

"I think we should go now," she says.

The first phase of my punishment is to have to break this news to Avery.

"What? Already? We just got here! I didn't finish my beer! I only had one dance!"

"Something happened."

"What?"

"It's hard to explain."

"What is it?"

"It's—it's a Japan thing."

—◻—

On the walk to the station, where we will go our separate ways, Avery asks Ayana for her phone number "in case you want to do something before I go back."

Ayana gives him *a* phone number.

I snare Avery with my conversational tractor beam, partly to spare Ayana from him and partly to spare myself from Ayana.

"I can't dance, as you may have noticed."

"What, are you kidding? That was *great!* What do you call it?"

"It's the Antler Dance."

"Well, everybody was doing it!"

"Really?"

"Yeah! Didn't you notice? They all started copying you, man!"

Ayana favors us with a brief word of corroboration.

"You're *money*, baby!" Avery assures me. "You are *so money* and you don't even know it!"

Then he adds, "Hey you guys—did I tell you I'm coming back to Japan in September? Can we do all this again then?"

—◻—

I send Ayana a brief email to thank her for helping me out with Avery.

Silence.

Summer vacation comes. My student helpers and I are recording the final tracks for my big new album to be released that fall.

To celebrate its completion, we all go to the annual fireworks display in Yamashita Park. I get drunk, lose my shoes there and ride the subway home barefoot. It becomes an NU urban legend. *What great ones do, the less will prattle of.*

It ought to be a fun summer, but Ayana's silence grows louder with every passing day.

As much as I want to believe that my daring dance-floor rescue cancelled out my earlier indiscretion, I come to realize, big duh, that I am kidding myself there. Finally, at summer's end, I tuck pride in the back of the sock drawer next to the penile suction pump and face reality.

The Japanese chick is endowed with a finite but measurable capacity for forgiveness. And I am endowed with an infinite capacity for groveling for their forgiveness. Especially in writing. This happy convergence of endowments has lubricated my relationships with Japanese chicks for going on two decades.

So let the groveling commence!

The email begins with a chatty account of my summer vacation, then veers toward the point:

I know you're upset about what I did to you at the club that night when Avery was here. I've thought about it a lot. I know it was terribly rude. I don't have any good excuse for my behavior. I'm sorry.

Please forgive me if you can. If you don't want to meet me in person any more, I would understand that. But I'm sure you are making a lot of preparations now for applying to grad schools in the US, and you might need help. If you'd at least keep in touch with me and let me advise you about that, I'd be very happy.

I miss you.

The reply comes the next day:

I thought about writing to you many times before, she begins.

There is a painful paragraph in which she expresses the depth of the shock she received that night. This is Ayana, after all. You don't get off lightly in her courtroom. But then there is this:

I know that I can't blame you completely. There were some times that I gave you the wrong impression. I noticed the way you looked at me, and I didn't discourage your way of thinking about me. Maybe you had some good reason to think that I wanted to be with you in that way.

Anyhow, I did appreciate getting your email. I'll think about what you wrote. As for my applications, I am working on a lot of things now. I may contact you about them later.

The very same day, I get an email from Avery. He is taking a great offer with this *money* new company so, sad to say, he will not be making his return trip to Japan after all.

Would I mind breaking this news to Ayana, he wonders.

3

The grad school applications did serve to bring us together again. But it was never really the same.

We had dinner about once a month. No heavy drinking, no innuendo, no cousins once removed. I myself stayed twice removed, even on crowded elevators. These were more like lawyer-client prison consultations than dates.

It was never the same. But it was better than nothing.

—◻—

My long penance spent ghost-writing her application essays and plodding through tedious admissions procedures on her behalf paid off; she was leaving for grad school in Oregon in a few weeks.

She wanted to meet one more time to express her gratitude—but on her own terms. Experience had taught her that NU faculty members were best met in well-lit locations with plenty of people around. We met on a Saturday afternoon at campus, where the spring festival was in full swing.

She came dressed for a firefight: a loose-fitting linen Vietnamese pantsuit, jet black, with blue-tinted John Lennon granny glasses. She looked good. She just kept on looking better and better. If she had stayed in my life another year, surely she would have achieved full-blown beauty.

We moved among the booths in the international food court and I occasionally succumbed to the siren come-ons of sales-chicks. I answered each inevitable "Is this your wife?" with a proud "Why, yes—yes she is!" Ayana's violent denials gradually faded to sighs.

We sat at a table under a beach umbrella to have surprisingly unatrocious boiled dumplings.

"Do you think you'll keep working here in NU?"

"Sure. Until I get fired."

"Why do you always say that? Do you really think they'll fire you?"

"It's always possible. I'm having way too much fun. Some professors hate people who have more fun than they have. And it's hard to get around that, because those people never have any fun at all."

"What if they don't fire you? Will you stay until you get old?"

"As long as I have NU chicks around me, I will never get old. And I'll never die."

Passing chicks waved cheerily to me, so I did not realize that Ayana was lost in thought until she said, with quiet amazement, "You really do believe that, don't you."

—◻—

Ayana saw an old friend she wanted to talk to. I remembered him. He was one of her California exchange-student buddies from two or three years before. I would have talked to him myself, but was distracted by two sophomore chicks trying to foist faux Thai curry on me, and was soon in the throes of giddy flirtation.

"That was Mike," Ayana said. "He got a job here in Japan."

"That's nice."

"We talked about that. And about *you*."

I shuddered. "What about me?"

"He used to watch you around campus when he went to school here," she said. "And then he was watching you just now with those two girls. He told me he wants to be just like you when he gets older."

"What's his job?"

"He teaches English at an all-girls' high school."

"Nice start!"

—◻—

I hugged Ayana goodbye and got home around two-thirty. At three, my nineteen-year-old lover came to visit.

That was a pretty good day.

LESSON 8

First, do no harm

"She a beagle true-bred, and one that adores me. What o' that?"
"I was adored once too."

—Twelfth Night

I did not have sexual relations with that woman.

1

"I really should be going home," I say after the movie, and she says why, and I say, "I just ought to go home," but she says it's still early so let's go to a coffee shop or something, and we duck into this little café by the station.

I order white wine; she has iced tea.

"I'm sorry the movie wasn't all that good," I say.

"No, it was okay."

But it wasn't. To toss Ewan McGregor, glam-rockers and orgies into a salad and have it turn out as tedious as Velvet Goldmine was a remarkable feat of filmmaking.

Still, scenes of such depravity that Japanese censors had blurred nearly the entire screen afforded me a chance to lean over and whisper, "Do you understand what's happening now? Would you like me to explain it to you?"—so at least I had the pleasure of making her blush.

"Perhaps another time, we'll see a good one," I say.

"Do you like me?"

"Yes, of course I like you."

She stretches a clammy hand across the table and I take it in mine. But my hand beats a cowardly retreat when the waitress returns.

"What do you like about me?"

HOW TO PICK UP JAPANESE CHICKS

Throughout her freshman year I met her and her twenty-seven classmates for ninety minutes four mornings a week.

By day our face-to-face contact was limited to "What do you have for Question Two, Miss Tsukamoto?" to which the response would either be the correct answer or an exasperated heaving of her upper body across her desk.

By night, the email came in. Every night. First it came as extra-credit English homework and then, when the language proved too confining for her, it came in Japanese.

Cascades of Japanese. Much of it was simple-minded; some of it was arrestingly insightful—by my standards, at least. Some of it was on politics, art, education; most of it was personal. All of it was honest, genuine, of the moment.

The fortress of cynicism that encased my middle-aged heart had no defense against this relentless siege of purity and openness. The walls tumbled; I began to respond in kind.

So insidiously that I did not notice, my daily reaction evolved from *Oh Lord, more blather from the pencil-necked geek?* to *Why hasn't she written yet today?*

—◻—

The appeal of her youth was a factor, no doubt. Many was the time I asked myself if I would have corresponded so fervently with a woman my—*Nope!*—own age, or with a male—*Nope!*—student who had sent me such intensely personal messages, and the answer[*] shot back even before the question was fully formed.

I say the appeal of her youth, not of her youthful beauty, for she did not possess physical beauty. Not, at least, by the lofty standards of NU.

---

[*] "Nope."

She had a tiny, delicate mouth—in that feature she certainly bettered Ayana—but it was lost in the comically broad flatlands of her face. An off-center widow's peak only added to its excessive geography. Her hair was dry enough to distress a fire marshal. One eye was set slightly higher than the other.

At school she wore glasses, little makeup, and clothes so frumpy and schoolmarmish that the long stretch of territory below her neck was open to broad speculation. It could have been Olive Oyl or Oprah under all that stuff.

Her neck…well now, that was splendid. Long and nearly as narrow as the stem of my wine goblet, it seemed incapable of supporting that unwieldy face. Indeed, two permanent horizontal creases testified to the burden it bore.

I complimented her on her neck every chance I got, and was always rewarded with a virginal blush. This wine was most definitely a rosé.

—◻—

Someday, when I have slaked my thirst for self-indulgent memoir writing, I will re-read her email correspondence in toto. I may even construct an index at some point to facilitate the research of future scholars of doomed intergenerational romance. Part of it might look like this:

abortion, 14, 159
  unwillingness to consider, 63
class party, 84-87
  need for organization of, 84
  unsuitability to be organizer, her, 85-86
  willingness to take on organizer's role if asked, her, 86
Clinton, Bill, 7, 33, 93-95, 172-75, 303, 511
  Northern Ireland troubles and, 101
  similarities with me 94, 213, 255-59, 377-79
English classes, my, 1-11, 22-26, 35-43, 81, 112-21, 297, 461-62

as sole reason for living, 79
ineffable excellence of, 80, 114-15, 177
gayness, my:
  assumption of at start of school year, 97
  disappointing lack of, as it would make me "the ideal man", 98
Hepburn, Audrey, 15-18, 248, 440-41
  rejection of neck comparisons with, 16
  reluctant acceptance of neck comparisons with, 18
homemade treats, her:
  ham-handed fishing for compliments on, 107-09
  supposed wretchedness of, 104
homepage, my, 28-30, 45, 111, 179, 233, 286, 389-90, 531
  unauthorized uploading of her picture and, 55
Japanese English teacher in charge of supplemental class:
  clear incompetence of, 27, 44, 131-35, 167, 198, 264
  necessity of summary execution of, 133
Nanking Massacre, 225-230, 266, 423-28
  cover-up of, 226
  need for improvement in junior-high history textbooks and, 230
  similar hidden atrocities and, 449
national flag, 292, 500-503, 528
  controversy over compulsory display of, 105
Northern Ireland, 93-95, 293, 402
  troubles in, 94-95
Radiohead:
  knack for encapsulating her feelings of self-loathing of, 77
  willingness to lend me albums, her, 78
rose-colored glasses, 12, 49, 473, 488
  overuse of by most people when recalling past events, 333
self-loathing, 22-24, 58-62, 77-78, 199-210, 341-68, 450-55, 504-10
  appearance and, 24, 58-59, 355, 506
  falling out with friend as cause of, 341-45, 361-68, 452
  recurrence of, 506-07
Streisand, Barbra, 186-88, 335-40
  iridescent charm of, 91, 337
US Air Force, 411-413, 514, 550
  childhood ambition to be a fighter pilot in, 411
Yoshiko, 1-5, 27-29, 44, 90-92, 122-127, 190, 251, 361-68, 452
  best-friend-for-life status of, 3, 27, 90, 125-26

shared hatred of Japanese English teacher by, 131-33, 167

—◻—

I did the math: She was born in the same week—possibly on the same day—that I first met Miss Hirano at the International House of English.

Her given name was Michiko. Miss Hirano's first name was, too.

—◻—

"What do you like about me?"

Earlier in the day I would have slam-dunked that one, but this is Hour Ten of our "date"—or outing, or take-our-daughters-to-porn day, or whatever this is—and I am not in shape for such a marathon.

Five, even three hours earlier, I could have deflected that question (It's the delicate, sweaty grip of your handshake) *or simply told the truth: for it was the utter her-ness of her that so enchanted me. At this stage, however, I could only hear the plaintive, distant whispers of my pillow, calling my bald and addled head home.*

—◻—

My third and final album went on sale at the fall school festival.

By local-artist standards, it was a triumph: over two hundred sold in two days, and nearly universal praise.

Michiko sent a cyber-review declaring the album "disappointing" and "surprisingly puerile."

It was as if one of my missionary great-aunts had come back to life and caught me window-peeping. I couldn't reply for a few days, then suggested that she might want to give it a few more listens before passing judgment.

She apologized for hurting me but wouldn't back down.

HOW TO PICK UP JAPANESE CHICKS

—◻—

The next Monday's mail topic was the movie *Gattaca*. She supported my nomination of it as one of the most underrated of all time. Notwithstanding that "all time" for her meant the second Clinton Administration, I was pleased to be in agreement with her on at least one aesthetic issue.

Tuesday's revisited a favorite theme: the consummate vileness of her homemade treats—which quickly reeled in a reassurance that my birthday cake was very tasty indeed.

On Wednesday came word of her mother's intention for her to attend a preliminary meeting for an arranged marriage with the rich thirty-three-year-old owner of a confectionery.

I groused that he seemed too young for her, but then proposed a way to make his death seem an accident so that we could make off with his fortune, and candy.

—◻—

I have a group photo of her class taken outside the bar after the obligatory class party, everyone ruddy-faced in the crisp November air and crammed together to fit into the frame.

Michiko is wearing her frumpy coat, a gray wool number from the June Cleaver collection. Her eyes are pink and puffy, anxiety attacks over the planning of the party having kept her up most of the night. But now, the bash getting rave reviews, she is the picture of teenage-chick bliss, despite the creepy bald white guy with the gray beard kissing her on the temple.

—◻—

I returned finals on her last day as a freshman. On the sparrow-like Yoshiko's exam, I had written:

I'm probably going to start having a love affair with your friend Michiko soon. I hope you won't hate me for it. I couldn't bear to be hated by you.

—◻—

That evening, I received an email inviting me to invite her on a *kenzen* date.

I'd never heard of such a thing, I wrote back.

Check your dictionary, she replied.

kenzen: wholesome, sensible

I said I'd never experienced a *kenzen* date, but that I would do my best.

—◻—

I hardly recognized her when she arose from a bench outside Yokohama Station to greet me. The geeky glasses were gone. She blinked frequently as she struggled with new contacts. Her makeup implied a bad day on the mini-paintball range.

—◻—

Ten hours later, as I sip my wine she asks, "Have you ever had a love affair with a student?"

I say, "I think I'm having one now."

2

By the start of Michiko's sophomore year, the worker bees in my internal Department of Conscience are logging eighty-hour weeks.

Their spokesman has evolved from that fuzzy gray character in a moldy courtroom drama to a fresher, more late-nineties gestalt. He takes the form of a pedantic, self-righteous incarnation of a tongue-cluck.

My internal DA has morphed into Dr. Phil.

—◻—

So you began sleeping with the girl from...when was it you said?

Early April, the start of her sophomore year, Dr. Phil.

Early April. And just how did that come about?

We were chatting on line one night while I worked my way through a bottle of wine. As so often happens late at night, my gonads seized control of the keyboard.

Your gonads...

I usually set the keyboard on my lap when I type. So you see, by virtue of proximity, my gonads easily wrest control of my typing away from my brain.

And what was it that your gonads communicated to her?

That I wanted her to come to my house again, as she had that very evening—but this time without Yoshiko. That I had trouble sleeping. That I wanted to lie down with her and fall asleep holding her in my arms.

And how did you feel when you sent that message?

Drunk. I mentioned the wine, didn't I?

Drunk.

It's sort of distracting when you repeat what I say, Dr. Phil. Yes, I was drunk.

Sort of distracting... Drunk... So that's your excuse?

No, I'm not making any excuse. The wine was just a facilitator, truth serum. I was getting nervous. She was dangling some mystery other-guy in front of me in her mail, and suddenly I realized how much I wanted to head off any competition. Wine enabled me to tell the truth.

The truth. And that was the whole truth, was it? About what you wanted to do, I mean.

Yes, Dr. Phil, it actually was the whole truth. At the time, I really wasn't thinking in terms of...

Intercourse?

Funny how that actually sounds dirtier than the word I was going to use.

So, if you weren't planning on having sex with the girl, what were *you planning?*

—◻—

Damned if I knew. And by this time, pretty well damned anyway.

—◻—

She has Saturday morning class this term and says she might drop by on her way home.

HOW TO PICK UP JAPANESE CHICKS

She comes in flouncing. It occurs to me that I have never used this word before, not even in internal monologue. And yet I know flouncing when I see it, and this is the very thing. We sip barley tea on my living room floor.

Talk turns to the day's class, one of the special courses needed to satisfy the requirement for a teacher's license.

"You really want to be a teacher?"

"I don't know."

"It seems like a lot of trouble taking all these extra classes if you're not sure."

"It's just a qualification."

"What do you mean?"

"A lot of people get the license even though they don't really plan to teach. It looks good on your résumé; helps you get all kinds of jobs."

"Oh. I didn't know that."

"You *should* know that."

I crawl into the tatami bedroom and slide beneath the blankets of the futon. I hold the blankets open, not saying a word.

She sighs a *so-he-really-means-it* sigh. She closes the sliding door, separating us. Two minutes later she reopens it, having changed into sweat pants and a t-shirt plucked from the depths of her shoulder-bag. She slides in with me.

I roll her into a spooning position. Her dry hair wafts into my nostrils, so I stroke it flat, then keep on stroking it. I can feel her teenage heart thrumming, racing around her ribcage like a gerbil watching the family cat close in.

I breathe deeply to calm myself as well as her. The scent of her hair is floral, vernal. Intoxicating. I circumnavigate her with my arms, locking fingers at her shoulder.

"You'd be a good teacher," I say.

"I don't think so."

"What would you teach, if you did?"

"Junior high social studies."

"You could tell them the truth about the war."

She goes into a spiel about bureaucratic restrictions on class content, and I actually fall asleep.

In an interlude of consciousness, I slide my hands down and cup her breasts, just firmly enough to get to know them. I doze off again.

Later, I cannot tell if she has slept or not.

We get up and eat some salads I have bought at the local deli for dinner while watching a lackluster would-be thriller in which Ewan McGregor works in a morgue.

I begin to despise Ewan McGregor.

—▫—

I feel I should apologize. My real intention was only to take a nap.

(True? I think so. This is my brain typing now, not my gonads.)

But of course, my behavior went a little beyond that.

I feel very good right now. Your presence was the best medicine for my mood. I can put the problems at school behind me and think about you, as if you were still here now. I'll sleep well tonight, and I hope you will too.

Today we made a memory that I will always cherish.

I sleep well indeed, and fortunately I begin to do so before this reply comes in:

You totally lied to me!
A friend would not do to a friend what you did to me!
You say you like me, but you really just want to fool around!
Just what am I to you, anyway? Don't treat me like a child!
I bet you won't sleep well now!

—▫—

HOW TO PICK UP JAPANESE CHICKS

It is my Sunday to take organist duty at church.

I mull responses during the four slow verses of "There Is a Green Hill Far Away."

What is this *Don't treat me like a child* business? I'm treating her the same as all the other chicks I've molested in a long and illustrious career.

Being of age, she should know legal precedent: if you don't register your revulsion on the spot—see *Ayana vs. Muggins* among others—you can't change your mind after dinner and a long, crappy movie.

Of course I drop the legalese when it comes time to reply and slip into my comfortable old whipped-boy sackcloth. I vow not to ask her to see me privately any more, and to strive to become the better person that she expects me to blah blah *blah* blah *blahhhh* blah blah blah…

The reply comes at dinnertime:

I guess I didn't get to the point in my last message, so you got confused. Sor-ree!

I was kind of embarrassed yesterday. Can you blame me? But today I'll tell you what I really think about it.

Should I write it? Do you really want to know?

Anyway, after you read this, delete it right away, okay? I'm dying of embarrassment!

Muggins… I'm not mad at you at all. And I don't want to break up with you. What I mean is, I can't *break up with you. I'd meet you again right now if I could!*

I think I like you ten times more than you like me.

Do you really think you could stop seeing me? You are sneaky. That's why I won't kiss you on the lips.

I love our time together!

I love it when we go out.

I love being in your room, just the two of us. It's the most comfortable place in the world for me.

I want to be with you more than with anybody else in the world! How about another "nap" together, and more fooling around?

I forgive you for being so horny. But if I don't cool you off sometimes, I'm afraid we'll end up with a baby!

—◻—

The following Saturday, I promise myself to be good in bed. Christian good, that is, or at least as close to Christian good as a forty-four-year-old educator can get while horizontal with a teenage student. And I succeed.

The bedroom curtains flutter in the spring breeze, allowing a few late-afternoon sunbeams to fleck the darkness. In these spotlights, dust motes perform a lazy ballet above the tatami stage on which we lie, intertwined, jabbering of this and that.

If it could just be like this forever, I think, wouldn't that be all right? Not *kenzen*. No, not *kenzen* by a long shot. But not eternally damning either…

Around four o'clock I excuse myself for a minute. When I return, I find the most beautiful sight I've ever seen awaiting me—and miss the last off-ramp on the Lost Highway.

—◻—

So, we're to gather that you're a Christian, a church-going man. Is that accurate?

I did my best, Dr. Phil.

You did your best. You were preying on this naïve, innocent teenager who was obviously just infatuated with her teacher, and you call that doing your best.

Is that a question?

I don't see how you could look yourself in the mirror. Or how you could sleep at night.

Sleeping, yes, was hard at first. Then it just became part of the cycle.

Pardon?

—◻—

The cycle:

Step 1: You take her out to a "safe" location—a date spot, to be sure, but one where the tomfoolery cannot get out of hand. Dinner in Chinatown, say, followed by a walk to Yamashita Park, some handholding by the pier with the sea breeze wafting in. Say goodbye at the station while inviting her over on Saturday. Get a noncommittal response.

Step 2: You greet her at the door on Saturday. Some desultory conversation. Then to bed. See her off to the bus stop so that she can get back to the family home in the suburbs before her curfew.

Step 3: You send warm email expressing your utter enchantment; you sleep like a…well, to avoid a cliché, like a sperm-depleted middle-aged English teacher.

Step 4: You wake up; you read hysterical, accusatory email denouncing your calculated exploitation.

Step 5: You send wimpy, groveling reply. Wait for reply to the reply. Toss and turn all night.

Step 6: You get up. Receive coquettish, flirting email concluding with promise/threat to track you down on campus for lunch.

Step 7: You have lunch in an empty classroom, if forty-five minutes of mooning and furtive handholding can be called lunch. Make plans for next outside date at a "safe" location.

Step 8: Repeat until sated, dead or fired.

— ◻ —

"What am I going to call you?"
"What do you mean, 'What are you going to call me'?"
"I can't just call you Muggins any more."
"You can't?"
"No. I have to have a name for you."
"Oh."
"Can I use your first name?"
"No. I'd find that inappropriate."
"Okay. How about *Muggy-chan*?"
"Do I get a vote on this?"
"No. You're Muggy-chan."
"I will come when called."
"What are you going to call me?"
"You know, I'm not good at making major decisions so soon after a major orgasm. At this age, I'm only good for one major event per hour. Good thing I'm not in any kind of position that carries responsibility. My God, how does that Clinton do it?"
"Come on! Pick a name!"
"Can't I call you Miss Tsukamoto?"
"Yuk!"
"But it excites me so to say it… Here, look."
"*Yuk!*"
"Okay, okay. Your family calls you 'princess,' right?"

"Yes, yes. *Michiko Hime-sama*, or sometimes they even say Princess Michiko in English."

"Thank God that's settled."

—◻—

Like Ayana before her, time makes her prettier.

Much of the improvement can be ascribed to the opening of those unexplored territories below her splendid neck. Plenty of pleasant surprises there. Renewable natural resources. Gifts that keep on giving.

Even features once deemed flaws—the asymmetric eyes, the off-center widow's peak—turn into powerful charms. The widow's peak becomes a favorite spot to plant a kiss. Not number one, but up there on the list.

Her hair is dry indeed, but always imbued with an irresistible vernal fragrance that will likely haunt my dreams to my dying day.

Those broad cheeks have become delightful playthings to be squeezed or tugged on whenever conversation wanes. It's even possible to scrunch them together and achieve cheek cleavage.

Yes, she keeps getting prettier by the day.

—◻—

"This feel good?"

"No."

"Well, how do *you* do it, then?"

A sigh.

She tutors my wrist in the correct procedure, speed and intensity—proving my point about her potential as a teacher.

"Is this better?"

"*Yes! Oooohhhh…*"

Till now my patented dial-phone technique had never let me down. *What's your phone number again? Four... oh... nine... three... eight... eight... six...*

But it is a whole new era and the old tricks don't work anymore. I have a touch-tone girl now.

"Haaaaaa!

"Ha-ha-HAAAAAA-ha-ha-ha-ha-HAAAAAAAA!"

And this delirious laughter during orgasms? What's up with that, anyway?

—◻—

"This is the really delicate part, right? What they call 'the package'?"

"Um, yes."

"Oh."

"And a lot of guys will really like it when you roll them around like that. But somehow it's never done anything for me."

"So I grab this thing here?"

"I prefer lower down."

"Like this?"

Within a month, she is able to administer a rip-snorting handjob southpaw while eating rice crackers and watching the six o'clock news. My little multitasking genius.

—◻—

Now, Mr. Muggins, it didn't occur to you, not even for a split second, that you might be exploiting this girl's naivety?

I will not have you call her a "girl," Dr. Phil. I insist you use the term "chick."

Fine, fine. Play your little word games. "This chick's naivety," then.

HOW TO PICK UP JAPANESE CHICKS

It's hard to feel like an exploiter when you're crawling around your own home naked on your hands and knees, trying to escape the armpit-tickling, rectum-probing fiend behind you.

So you're saying that you *were the exploited one? Is that it?*

No, that's not it. But one thing should be clarified: at least I never tried to stick random objects in her rectum. What's up with that, anyway, Dr. Phil? You supposedly being a psychologist and all… What does it symbolize when a chick does that to a man?

Let's face some hard facts. It's pretty obvious that all you cared about here was your own sexual gratification. And the added thrill of getting that gratification with a much younger woman. A child, really—not yet allowed to vote or drink alcohol.

True, but Japanese law is quirky. The drinking age isn't enforced, and from eighteen you can appear in adult videos.

Let's not get bogged down in legal minutiae.

Well, you're the one playing DA here, Dr. Phil.

The point is, you were using her for your own purposes.

With all due respect, Dr. Phil…

—¤—

You weren't there. You don't know.

    You weren't there in my room with us. You weren't there on the dates with us. You certainly weren't there inside my head, where night after night I kept saying, *Don't harm the girl. Don't harm the girl. Whatever you do, don't harm the girl.*

Sometimes I woke up saying it out loud.

I mantra-ed myself back to sleep with it.

And it's easy, Dr. Phil, oh so easy for you, with your wife of eight hundred seventy-six years or whatever it is, to talk about making the right choices, but out here on the other side of the camera it's not that simple.

—◻—

You were a quarter century older than the girl. Did that fact not enter your head at any time?

Twenty-four years! Not a quarter century!

It was twenty-five between your birthday and hers.

A petty matter of three months. And in five years, people no longer could have said "She's less than half your age." I worked it out.

Mr. Muggins—Josh—it just wasn't going to work out. It was doomed from the start. You knew that, didn't you?

I knew that. And I tried to tell her so. I tried.

—◻—

Michiko Hime-sama awakens in a blue moonbeam and gives me that bewildered how-did-I-get-here gaze again.

Only my right arm, which has slithered into its favorite position (under the Hepburnesque neck, over the arm, tangential to the breast), shares the light with her. My face is buried in a darkness that neatly foreshadows the horrid, black fate that awaits my soul. And yet even with my visage obscured she can somehow sense my mood.

"You're hard again *already*?"

"You inspire me."

"I should go home."

"You keep saying that. Nobody's stopping you."

"I thought guys your age weren't this...frisky."

"I wouldn't know. I haven't slept with guys my age."

"I wonder if my dad still gets hard this often."

"I wish you wouldn't think out loud so much. You're breaking my mood."

"Good."

"Anyway, you'd better get used to, uh, friskiness in a guy."

"Why?"

"Because guys your own age have got plenty of it."

"That's why I don't want a guy my own age."

"Then why don't you stay over more often? My friskiness would decline if I had more chances to—How shall I put this delicately?—spew it all over you in a big gunky mess."

"...I really should go home."

"Uh-huh. You really should."

"Do you use Viagra?"

"*You* are my Viagra."

She sighs and rolls onto her side.

"It's late. Tell me a story, Muggy-chan."

"A bedtime story? You want me to put you to sleep?"

"At your age, I figure it'll put *you* to sleep."

—◻—

Just tell me this: Did you love her?

Yes, I did, Dr. Phil. I told her so. Often. And easily. It felt right whenever I said it.

What does love mean?

Is this a trick question?

I can see you have not read my recent book—

Stow that, now. You have plenty of opportunities for plugging on your own time. Your role in this fantasy is to torment me, to force me to face harsh realities. Don't try to weasel out of it.

The point is, to love someone is to care about them more than you care about yourself. It means doing the right thing for that person, even if it hurts you deeply and—

Excuse me, but could you possibly speak a little faster? Maybe not drawl quite so much?

—even if it hurts you deeply, and even if, in the short run, it hurts that other person. Can you honestly say that you acted in such a manner with this young woman?

That's a good question, Dr. Phil.

Thank you.

—◻—

Unlike Macbeth—and I can't speak for Bill Clinton—I was a man wading into sin with his eyes wide open.

No trio of witches cast a spell on me. There were no trite excuses ("It just happened") or finger-pointing at organs that can't speak up in their own defense ("The heart wants what it wants"). There were no passive verbs in my private thoughts, no parsing of phrases. I knew what "is" was.

Every day throughout the world, hundreds of college chicks throw down the gauntlet of flirtation in front of hundreds of male faculty. Most, I'm assuming, choose not to pick it up. I chose to pick mine up.

I took it home and watered it—and yes I know this is a pureed metaphor because you don't usually water gauntlets, but let's just say that you do because it's been a long day—and I made it grow. I could have clipped it at any time before it bloomed to full flower; could have killed it, for that matter, even after it did.

But I chose not to.

I rationalized, for a while, that to nip it in the bud would hurt her more than anything else could. But as Dr. Phil so rightly points out, damn him, short-term pain then would have spared both of us a lot more later on.

—◻—

Summer.

Let me enjoy my flower for one summer. God—Dr. Phil—Great-grandfather—Obi-wan—anybody else who might judge me—please let me have this one summer, and then I'll break it off, and I'll be a good boy, I promise.

This was the very year that Japanese ladies of my generation were salivating all over their translations of *The Bridges of Madison County*. Some even went on package tours to the middle of Iowa to tie ribbons on the actual bridges.

What makes a lonely farm wife's adultery with a transient photographer—who turns out to be creaky old Clint Eastwood in the movie, for heaven's sake—so acceptable, even commendable? What has *that* story got that mine doesn't?

Who wrote these rules, anyway?

3

"Let's have another dinner party here."
"Okay. Let's."

"I want to make *okonomiyaki*."

"You can do that? Here?"

"Sure. All we need is something to fry on."

"I have frying pans."

"They're too small. And filthy. I'll bring what I need from home."

—◻—

We have dinner parties with her girlfriends.

They blab nonstop from the moment they arrive, ignore the host, manage to get wildly drunk and yet invariably leave the apartment cleaner than they found it.

The Princess always arrives before the others. We go shopping for ingredients together. She sets about making the initial preparations before the others arrive—or tries to do so while I molest her.

On one occasion, she sighs with resignation and leads me into the bedroom for a quick one, just so she can get back to the cutting board. I will reek of raw onions all night.

I consider posting a sign in the kitchen:

Employees must wash hands after anal probing.

—◻—

As a ritual, a picture is taken at each party to immortalize the gorgeous spread just before we start to devour it. It's like the moment of pride that Tibetan monks might allow themselves before sweeping away a painstakingly constructed sand mandala, crossed with the scene from *Little Women* after Father has come back from the war. The Princess and I sit at the head of the cluttered table. The girls attend us, waiting for our permission to dig in.

After the main course, there may be game playing, or I might take to the keyboard and sing songs from my albums.

They lie on the floor and help themselves to pillows and coverlets. Then I serve Häagen Dazs for dessert.

I start to wonder how much the others know. When the Princess chases me around the apartment rendering me helpless with precision tickling attacks, what do they make of that? Does it not strike them a bit odd that their classmate should possess such an intimate schematic of the English teacher's sensitive zones?

—¤—

Five of us go to the annual fireworks at Yamashita Park that July. The Princess wears a *yukata*, the traditional light kimono for summer. She looks sexy in it. Experience is giving her confidence; confidence is giving her sex appeal.

She invites a friend from high school. The friend has been studying in the Great Satan and has not seen the Princess for over a year. The friend sees everything instantly.

The other friends, the NU chicks, have been there throughout the whole slow process. For them it has been like watching a beard grow in real time.

For the friend back from the Satan, the beard is suddenly *there*, and sprouting from an impossible place—an elbow, maybe, or a kneecap.

She sees the change in the Princess and sees the reason for it—seems to see every single thing we've done. Watching her watch us, I can hear the tumblers clicking into place: disbelief at first, a barely suppressed revulsion, then a begrudging acceptance—or perhaps just a polite desire not to upset a festive occasion.

Will the others react the same way when they find out?

—¤—

Okay, I can see there's no use appealing to your concern for others. Let's talk about your self-interest.

Fine.

Did you like your job?

I loved my job.

Oh, really?

Dr. Phil, have you been paying attention? My job was virtually my life before the Princess came along. Have you heard me talk about a social life with friends my own age? Get a clue.

I just have to wonder how much you cared about your job, since you so easily put it all at risk.

We took some precautions.

Such as?

The no-PDA rule.

What does that mean?

"Public Displays of Affection." Where did you get your degree again?

Never mind that.

We didn't grope each other at school. Later, I had to declare the five-kilometer radius around my apartment a grope-free zone. It just wouldn't do to have her stroking my hand in a coffee shop, or sucking on my fingers at the local Denny's and have, say, the office secretary walk by.

She sucked on your fingers? At Denny's?

Jealous, Dr. Phil?

You were playing with fire letting her engage in such behavior anywhere.

I know. And we *were* seen. People would come up and say, "I saw you at the zoo last weekend with a woman. You looked so happy. Was that your wife?"

And how did you reply?

Sheepishly.

Playing with fire, I repeat.

—◻—

"Suppose the dean calls you into his office one day, like this sniveling prosecutor who's after my man Clinton," I say. "He tells you that some of the students feel uncomfortable because they've seen you and Mr. Muggins together behaving as much more than just friends. Then he asks, 'Do you have something to tell us?' What would you say?"

"I would say," she responds instantly, "'You're in no position to ask that question, Dean Asada.'"

Good point. The whole Department of International Relations is a veritable lawnful of Hummel-like mini-Clintons, all tenured for life, unimpeachable. Studentosexual impulses are rampant and not always suppressed. If I do end up boiling in the Batshit Jacuzzi in Hell I'll see a lot of familiar faces around me, and then we'll really test the old adage about misery loving company.

One day I'm told that my colleagues have indeed been watching me. Hints are dropped that I will soon succeed Mr. Furman as coordinator of the English program. The wages of sin, it seems to me, are pretty darn good.

4

I think I'll stay home today…

Yes, that's what I'll do. I'll catch up on my lesson prep for fall semester.

Then the phone rings. The Princess wants to go to the park. I say it's too hot out, why not come over here? She says no, she has another plan in the evening but she wants me to kill time with her in the park till then.

She figures I'll cave.

I cave.

—ロ—

I stand at the usual place. It's a bank of coin lockers at the far end of Yokohama Station, where the commuter line ferries her into the city. I watch columns of wilting hominids stream through the ticket gates, blur together into massive clots and finally dissolve into tendrils that slowly untangle, revealing her.

There she is in jeans and a white blouse, picking up speed as she sees me, flouncing again, that huge head wobbling tenuously atop that skinny neck, her every molecule exuding a pure and simple love. I move toward her, arms open.

Even though it has happened so many times before and will happen unknowable times more, it feels miraculous. Surely the sight of the Holy Spirit descending from Heaven could not be more moving.

In boyhood I had a terrier that mourned for me when I went off to college. Whenever I returned home, it rushed to the door and urinated on the spot.

I am now the terrier, with only slightly better bladder control.

—□—

We spread a couple of beach towels in a deeply shaded section of the park. It's cool here, evergreen cool, spearmint gum cool, and glints of the ocean shimmer through the trees.

We eat our sandwiches. We drink our tea. We loll. We've got lolling down to an art form by now.

She rolls onto her stomach. As usual, her blouse is too plain to be sexy; in fact it's almost—here's that word again—schoolmarmish. Sensing my disappointment, she undoes a few buttons. She invites me in.

I hesitate at first. Families stroll nearby occasionally. A gaijin lady is propped up against a cherry tree not far away and will see us if she looks up from her book.

I reach in and caress one of them, then the other. Her bra is still on, but then she does that magic trick that she does, unsnapping it and dragging it out through an armhole one-handed.

I suggest we get a room. Maybe it's my own idea or maybe it's telepathic input from the gaijin lady, but it sounds like a good idea. I know where a room can be gotten because I've long ago done recon on the Yamashita Park area.

"It wouldn't do any good," she says.

"Why not?"

"I couldn't do it even if I wanted to."

"Why not?" I repeat, but I know. Her cycle is one of her few predictable attributes.

"I'm a *girrrrrrrrl*, that's why!" And she rolls over, tumbling into my arms, without letting my hand escape its sublime trap.

—◻—

It's time for her to head off to her other appointment. One of her high school teachers plays guitar in an amateur soft-rock band that's doing an outdoor gig in Sakuragi-cho, down by the pier, and she has promised to be there.

I'm not going to turn her over to another musically inclined pedagogue while she's in this frame of mind. I invite myself along.

We walk the Motomachi shopping arcade from the park to Ishikawa-cho Station. It has a quaint European old-town flavor to it, as it was once the foreign enclave of Yokohama in missionary days. Great-grandfather likely trod these very streets.

I see a familiar face. It's Wakako, a girl from the class one year ahead of hers.

I drag the Princess into a Baskin-Robbins, trying to convince myself that I am not hiding but just suddenly feel like ice cream. As I am easily duped, I succeed.

We lap away at sugar cones facing a mirrored wall.

When we were new, I hated mirrors. We might be browsing in a department store when suddenly our reflection would leap out from a mirror and smack me in the forehead, forcing me in that moment to see us the way the world did:

Gray-bearded gaijin in his forties—maybe even his fifties, who can tell with those people?—with some innocent young thing… What's the story there?

I am marveling at the lack of that feeling now. When did it expire? A long time ago, and quietly. We look just fine together now.

HOW TO PICK UP JAPANESE CHICKS

—□—

Now we're at the station, waiting on a small metal bench.

She's really getting squirrelly now, going for all my ticklish zones—armpits, ribs, love handles… And I'm retaliating in my usual manner, snatching at whatever piece of her re-installed bra that I can get a grip on to snap her with.

Then there's the sensation of being watched, and I see Wakako coming down the platform toward us.

I rise to head her off.

"I think I saw you at the jewelry store back there—ha-ha-ha!" I say, the laugh sounding as if read from a teleprompter. "But you looked busy, so I didn't want to bother you!"

I am keenly aware that I am exclaiming but can't stop it.

Wakako ignores my blisteringly droll repartee. She cranes to see beyond me.

"Where are you going? Sakuragi-cho?" I ask, hoping it is not so.

"No, Yokohama Station. Is that your wife?"

"My wife?"

Okay. Here it is. It is the moment I have long been preparing for.

I would deal out the plain truth and let the chips fall where they might. *That's my girlfriend*, I would say. *That's the woman I love. And she's about your age—younger actually—and what are you going to do about it?*

"No. No, that's not my wife."

"A relative?"

"Uh, no…"

Wakako is a big girl. Trying to block her view is like elbowing Shaq out of the paint. "Who is she, then?"

"That's…that's a sophomore."

"Oh."

Then did the cock crow a second time.

Josh Muggins

—◻—

It's not a bad band, really, but it's best experienced as an echo.

They are playing in a little arcade that I had never noticed on prior trips to the pier. It's tucked down by the sea, hidden from view by a huge four-masted sailing ship that is preserved there as a tourist attraction.

The concert is part of some kind of charity festival. Little stands are selling fried octopus, yakitori, drinks.

At first we sit at a picnic table in front of the band where her teacher can see her, and we eat what will pass for dinner. Then we climb over a low hill to enjoy each other for dessert.

The band takes on a ghostly reverb with the top of the hill between them and us. On our side, we look down a gentle slope dotted with couples and families. Everyone is here for the view.

A canal that runs to the ocean sparkles before us. The ocean itself twinkles in the distance under the declining sun. In between, there is Cosmo World, the mini-amusement park. The distant screams of roller coaster passengers intermittently drown out the band's phantomy chords. There is a haunted house over there, and games, and numerous rides for all ages, all overshadowed by what was until recently the world's largest Ferris wheel.

She's less demonstrative here on the knoll, and I'm grateful for the break. Her heart is always racing at a million beats a minute, but now, for once, it slows down to my pace. She's content to lie still and enjoy the view while I stroke her hair and enjoy the view of her. I'm Helen Keller, reading her forehead, her hairline, her ears, her chin, her neck.

This continues for a million years.

—◻—

We decide to hit Cosmo World.

The haunted house is first. It sucks and is good for laughs.

Then the roller coaster. I can see what the squeals were all about. It's not much to look at, but for sheer torque, for the sheer giddiness born of wondering *When did this thing last have maintenance?*, it beats anything Disney has to offer.

The Princess is white knuckled. I'm laughing so manically that she stares at me, but it doesn't deter me.

Hey, you do it during orgasms. I do it on roller coasters.

—◻—

The Ferris wheel never stops. It moves so slowly, it doesn't have to. The cars—enclosed carriages—swoop down to the platform at so stately a pace that the couple or family inside can easily scamper out and let the next occupants take over.

The carriages are red, green, blue. We bet on which color we'll get. I say blue, but we get red. The nice elderly couple behind us gets blue.

We can see the elderly couple through our back window as we ascend. They might be in their eighties. We wave. They wave back. No signs of judgment. From their perspective the chasm between forty-four and nineteen is a puddle-jump.

As we approach the nine o'clock position on our clockwise climb, we notice that we have pulled out of view of our neighbors. We do what comes naturally to us in such circumstances.

Nature has done its best to thwart us on this day, but we find a way around Nature.

By the time we near twelve o'clock high, we are most gratified.

And now the whole city is coming into view on one side, gradually lighting itself, an endless panorama of fireflies. On the other side, the sun sinks into the ocean, painting all our carriages purple, and all our thoughts too.

And still we keep going up, up, ever upward. And then there's our moment at the top. On a fast ride, one feels momentarily weightless up here. In slow motion the sensation is subtler but lasts longer.

It's perfect. This is the top of the ride, you suddenly realize. This is the top of the *whole* ride. The biggest of them all.

And it's all downhill from here.

LESSON 9

Reality is not your friend

Every now and then a student will develop an infatuation with a teacher, either as a romantic interest or as an academic role model. This situation can give rise to damaging rumors and hurt your academic career, so it is crucial to head off the problem when it first arises.

—Faculty handbook

*Every now and then we hear our song
We've been having fun all summer long*

—The Beach Boys

1

Okay. So your Bridges of Madison County *summer came to an end.*

Yes.

And so you ended the relationship? As you said you would?

Well…

Okay, now what?

The thing is, she enrolled in my TOEFL intensive course in mid-September.

Say what?

I couldn't dump her and then have her in class all day. Imagine you dumping your wife, Dr. Phil—though I gather from last night's tender whisperings that the opposite is more likely—and then imagine that she's *still* sitting in your studio audience every day for the next week. That's what it would have been like if I had dumped the Princess at the end of August, before she took TOEFL intensive.

What is this "TOEFL" that you keep talking about?

The Test of English as a Foreign Language. Essentially it's the SAT if you're a foreigner who wants to go to an American university.

All right, I got it.

So it was a prep class for people who wanted to take that test and eventually study abroad.

Uh-huh.

I threw old editions of the real exam at them every day. Fascinating stuff, really. All the readings are taken out of college texts—largely natural sciences, the kinds of subjects that I put off taking until my sixth year in college.

I see.

There was this mesmerizing passage about the way scientists study the dietary preferences of bald eagles. I used that one so often that I nearly memorized it. Turns out they have a technique called "pellet analysis."

Ah.

See, after the bald eagle devours its prey, the indigestible parts congeal into a pellet. Now, you would think that the eagle would expel this pellet in the usual way, but you would be wrong.

Would I?

Oh, yes. The eagle instead vomits the pellet out its beak. Intrepid researchers venture up to the nest to retrieve such pellets, which are then subjected to analysis to determine their composition. That's how they know what the bald eagle has been eating.

That's quite enough.

But you see, it's not entirely accurate because some food items, such as sinewy, furry rodents, are less easily digested than—

ENOUGH!

—¤—

Sorry. You get met started on the bald eagle diet and it happens every time.

Who got you started?

The point is, she was taking this intensive class. Which I loved teaching. You get twenty-five people who willingly subject themselves to the bald eagle *and* the bald teacher for a whole week and earn not a single credit! Six hours a day in class, almost as many for homework... And after they pass the exchange selection, they *thank* you for torturing them. If you're a language teacher, it doesn't get any sweeter than that.

All right. So this girl took your class because she wanted to study abroad. Is that right?

No. Sorry to say, but no.

Then why?

Because I was teaching it. She would have taken Intermediate Embalming had I offered a section of it.

You're sure that's the reason?

Look, *I* wanted her to do a year abroad more than she did. It would have been best for both of us. Her departure would have given us an automatic break. So yes, I wanted her to go. Even more so after that class. On all the mock tests she got the highest score in the group and really could have qualified for the exchange program if she'd applied.

You sound proud.

Did I mention the scholarship? She was one of only three students in her whole department that year to qualify for a grade-based tuition reduction, despite the B I stuck her with.

Are you this girl's lover or her father?

Can't I do both?

Sorry. Neither.

—◻—

But creepy as it sounds, I had both feelings. Never simultaneously, but often within hours of each other.

After a long day in TOEFL class, we would walk down the hill toward the station, often hand in hand. The PDA rule…well, it was more of a guideline at this stage. Later that night, I would check her test results and the father feeling would wash over me. My God, she was magnificent!

I couldn't dump her while she was taking that class, Dr. Phil. Think of her test scores!

— ◻ —

"I thought," I say, "that Mr. Furman was guaranteed another two-year extension under the rules."

"It's more of a guideline than a rule," says Professor Twain. "And we simply can't put up with him anymore."

"I really like the job I have now."

"The faculty have made their decision. Furman will be paralyzed with Amazonian darts while we all wait our turn to shit in his mouth."

No, that's a lie. Professor Twain is far too fine a Christian and gentleman to say such a thing.

"Most of the faculty don't even know me," I say.

"But they know Furman all too well. And they do know you—by reputation."

Professor Twain, one of the few tenured non-Japanese on the faculty, has been deputized by his brethren to strong-arm me.

"But this coordinator position is management," I whine. "I've never done that. I wouldn't be good at it."

"How do you know?"

"Believe me. When it comes to managing things, well…"

Professor Twain leaves my ellipses hanging in the air while I try to measure how much truth he can be trusted with.

"There's just a lot about me that you don't know," I say. "I could end up embarrassing everybody. And besides," I astound myself by adding, "Furman's not doing that badly."

"Many of us are fed up with his antics," Professor Twain says, stroking his neat blond goatee. "The other day I had the most unpleasant meeting with him that I can ever remember having with a colleague. He just doesn't know how to *behave*."

He wheezes at the unpleasant memory.

"The feeling among the faculty," he concludes, "is that you're much more of a grownup."

—◻—

"Muggins!" calls out Satsuki, elfin duet partner and co-producer of my latest album. I adore her. But I approach with caution. Her tone is that of Miss Gulch, come to snatch Toto away from me.

There is no scene on earth as beautiful as our campus during a lunch hour in the fall. The sun, offset by a soft, crisp breeze, rules an almost painfully azure sky, under which hundreds of our denizens enjoy lunch on the grass.

With but six words—"We heard about you from Wakako"—Satsuki creates winter in October.

"What do you mean?"

But I know.

"Wakako. You know. Last summer. She saw you. At Ishikawa-cho Station."

—◻—

"I do want to stay over," she is saying, "but I don't know. Sometimes it's creepy."

"Creepy? My dear child, you cut me to the quick."

"Not you, Muggy-chan." She has started to pronounce the nickname with a lilt, suggesting a Japanese Southern belle. "But when I go out in the morning, even really early, there's always this weird lady hanging around. And she glares at me."

"What does she look like?"

She describes my landlady, who attends Community Outreach lectures at school and is chummy with my dean. Yow.

It's time to become a man, and put away childish things.

HOW TO PICK UP JAPANESE CHICKS

—◻—

I email her to meet me in a coffee shop near the station after class.

I have scouted this location as the most suitable one for public hysteria: tables set well apart from one another, usually not crowded.

This will be the day.

But she shows up in that black dress. A better writer could give it the description is deserves, could provide all the usual details of the fabric, the cut, the print. But then again, that writer would be gay and therefore not telling this story.

All I can say is that there is, again, something of the old-time Southern Belle about her whenever she wears it. It made its debut one memorable summer date. It inspires me, renders me helpless, and she knows it.

The season for it has passed, but it is warm for an October day, and she wears it into the coffee shop.

Let's go to my place, I hear someone say. That's me again, all right.

Sure, someone else says. That would be her.

—◻—

"Talk dirty to me, Muggy-chan" she says.

Of course I oblige. I describe to her the main event that will soon follow, emphasizing its slowness, its tenderness, its predestined gooiness. I wonder if I'm doing this right.

She moans. Good sign.

I pause to kiss a breast, then return to nibbling on an earlobe.

I express an intention to torture her with teasing and false starts until she asks for it, begs for it. And then, I say, I'll seem to acquiesce to her pleading, but not so, and make her beg some more.

She gasps. There may be no need to carry out the things I describe; the play-by-play alone is enough for her. It may well be enough for me, for that matter.

I talk her through the nasty deed like the Control Tower in one of those dreadful movies in which an amateur ends up landing a jetliner. I explain the precise sequence of movements I expect of her fingers and her mouth, and the involuntary reactions she will surely exhibit and—

The phone rings.

—◻—

It's the manager of the International Exchange Center at school. He's in charge of the TOEFL intensive courses.

The mood already shattered, I pick up.

He has heard that I am about to sign a contract that will upgrade my status on the faculty. He regrets to inform me that, under university rules, my compensation for future TOEFL intensive courses will therefore be cut by two-thirds.

A heated exchange follows. I was counting on full payment for those courses above and beyond all the goodies that Professor Twain had enumerated when he finally swayed me. I hang up, panting with disgust and anger.

"You should have expected that," she says.

"What?"

"It's just common sense. You were like a 'temp' before, and now you're a regular employee. You don't get the perks of a temp now."

"How do *you* know about this kind of thing?"

"Like I said, common sense."

I stare at her, fury and paternal pride wrestling for supremacy in my mind.

"Okay, okay," she says. "Come here. I'll make it better."

I weigh the day's events. On the one hand, seven thousand dollars in annual income up in smoke. On the other, naked and willing teenager on my carpet.

Life in Japan is a Monopoly board, I think, not for the first time, in which every square is Chance or Community Chest.

—◻—

Not every day could be a black dress day.

True, but I couldn't take any chances. She had an arsenal of weapons and knew all my weak spots. So I dumped her by email.

That's pretty cowardly.

That's what she said.

Exactly what did you say?

It's not worth quoting. Like most things I write it started off swimmingly, then lost the reader's attention halfway through and earned a rotten review.

You did the right thing, you know.

Did I? At one point, I believe I said, "This has been a marvelous carnival ride, but it's making me dizzy. I have to get off it now."

Not good. Not good.

Well, I'd never done this before. Never in my life had I written this kind of message. To be sure, I had plenty of them on file for reference, but I had never composed one.

What was her reaction?

A terse message seething with hatred. A demand that I delete my entire file of our email exchanges and any other traces of our relationship—and all traces of my earthly existence, while I was at it.

And that was it?

I tried to smooth it over. God help me, I actually found myself using that "Let's-still-be-friends" chestnut that chicks always toss out on these occasions. Big surprise: it doesn't work any better when the male uses it.

Awkward though it was, late though it surely was, it was still the right thing.

Yeah. Sure.

Teaching Point 16: Never compare a chick to a carnival ride. They really don't like that.

2

"Exercise B, number one. What's your answer?"
Silence.
"Anybody? I'll give you one point if you get it right."
Silence.
"Okay, three points."
Silence.
Now this is nice, I tell myself. *With the chick out of your head, you can concentrate more. You can prep your lessons better. You can really start to dig your spurs into these remedials.*
"How about you Yusuke?"

"I don't know."

"Takayuki?"

Silent, trout-like lip movements.

"Plant Man?"

"No idea."

"See, now, this is why you're in remedial class. Because you're all totally stupid."

You're so much better off now, I keep telling myself.

—◻—

If only Creative Excuse Writing were a credit-bearing course, they all would have been off the hook.

Plant Man—so named for his constant physical presence combined with an utter lack of sentient behavior—and his caretaker Yusuke are innocent men, wrongly failed by an evil teacher who played favorites with the girls in his class. So they deserve some slack, don't they?

Masaki works every night at a bar and doesn't get home till three, so it's just too hard to get up for an early afternoon class. I understand, right?

Akira famously plunged from the fourth-floor balcony of his girlfriend's apartment, shattering his leg in four places. If he is faking his limp and scars, he deserves both free credits and a Tony.

And then there is poor, sad Takayuki, a lost sheep among the wolves. Pale, bespectacled, rail-thin, utterly hairless south of the eyelashes (one could assume), he owns the image that adorns the dictionary definition of *pipsqueak*. I pray for his sake that he is gay because it is obvious that he will never know the inside of a woman.

He may have answered some of my questions in class correctly. No one can tell. His lips move, but no sound comes out. He always appears to be the ventriloquist's dummy of whoever happens to sit next to him.

On the last day of the first term, still woefully short of points, he approaches me after class.

"I really need to get credits for this class in both semesters."

"Well, I'm sorry, but you've failed this one. Try again in spring term."

"My parents will be angry."

"Yes, but you only came to half the classes and hardly did any work."

Up close in an empty room he is audible, but barely. Words gush out of him in spurts.

"Had-to-go-to-the-hospital-every-day... Psychiatrist... Treating-me-for-depression... Family-is-not-kind-to-me... Must-stay-here... Can't-go-home-if-I fail..."

I tell him I'll think about it and dismiss him. His tobacco breath is making me dizzy.

I check out his story in the registrar's office. A gruff female bureaucrat softens at the mention of his name. *Yes, yes, what a pitiful case it is. That poor little dear.*

I track Takayuki to his natural habitat, the designated smoking area of Building Six.

"Okay, here's the deal," I say. "I'll give you a passing grade. But you start the next semester ten points in the hole. Deal?"

"But... Hospital... Therapy... Must-go-every-day..."

"*Deal?*"

"O—okay."

I will never see him in class again.

—◻—

So it really was over then? You didn't knuckle under to temptation? You let her be? You maintained your dignity as a member of the faculty?

Oh, Dr. Phil, if only I'd had some to begin with.

Hard to believe Tom Hanks was ever that young.

But there he is, washed up on the beach in a tattered tuxedo, trying to cope with a raging hangover and the jumpy naked chick hiding in the bushes. I'm relating on so many levels.

I have "English through Cinema" in Room 214 on Wednesday afternoon, and we're using the old mermaid comedy *Splash!* this term.

It's a noncredit course, but she paid three thousand yen for it. It seems such a waste. And I know she'd like this movie if she ever showed up.

"If you prefer that I not call on you, fine," I write. "But I mean really—three thousand yen."

For the next three Wednesdays there is a surly shadow in the back row.

I'm taking questions on the script for Scene Ten. An innocent freshman girl in front calls my attention to the segment in which Tom reminds Daryl Hannah about the times they have "done it" in the car, in the elevator and on top of the refrigerator; she wants me to explain the unstated antecedent of this "it."

My gaze locks into the Princess's; she's reveling in my sweaty discomfort.

Five minutes after the bell, she will be chasing me around the classroom, lunging for my armpits while her mystified classmates trickle out.

3

I move into Mr. Furman's office. That is to say, we move in. It's in a building at the opposite end of campus from all my faculty colleagues, which suits me—us—fine.

She gives me a vase full of artificial flowers. I give her a copy of the key. Suddenly: "Hiroe's not a virgin."

"Gee," I say, "should we call CNN?"

"You already knew that? How?"

"I've met her boyfriend," I say. "I know he exists."

Yes, he exists, in his singularly vapid way. His function on earth might be to refute the syllogism *I think, therefore I am.*

Hiroe, recently handed the best-friend-for-life portfolio previously held by the sparrow-like Yoshiko—chick politics is brutal—deserves better. But why are we discussing this?

"We were in Psych and the lecture was really boring, so I passed her a note that I wrote in English: *Are you a virgin?* And she handed it back with *No* on it."

Okay, okay. I'm slow, but now I get it. Hiroe's boyfriend, cauterized brain stem notwithstanding, is at least a socially presentable boyfriend—walking proof of nonvirginity.

I age, therefore I am not.

—◻—

"Let's make a list," I say, "of what you require in a boyfriend."

"Why?"

"Just humor me. How about a car? You need a car?"

"A car?... No, that doesn't matter."

"Good, because most guys around here don't have one."

"Why are we—"

"Muscles? You need a big, strong guy?"

"No, not really."

"Work with me here. I'm not getting much of a picture."

She reaches across the restaurant table and seizes my jaw.

"Are you trying to get rid of me?"

"Nurr."

"I don't understand what I am to you."

"Yurr urrvurrtung."

I pry her hand off my face.

"You're everything."

"I don't know if I can trust you."

"I don't, either."

"You're a bad man, aren't you."

I want to drag out my old *I'm just a very bad wizard* comeback, but she would not get the culture-bound reference, and I'd just feel even older.

"Muggy-chan," she sighs, "I'm never going to leave you."

I hear thunder, or perhaps Dr. Phil slapping his pate.

—¤—

I start doing web searches on *infatuation*.

I try *infatuation AND causes*. I try *infatuation AND college women*.

Infatuation AND older man.

Infatuation AND teacher.

Infatuation AND rectal poking.

I am getting nowhere.

I leaf through the faculty handbook for advice:

…If you discover that a particular student takes up most of your office time, frequently calls you at home, and arranges to be in your path when you cross campus…

Yes? Yes? Oh, speak of that!

…you should take action to reduce the intensity of that interest.

Oh…bully.

Okay… What if the student comes flouncing into your private office, throws her arms around you, thrusts her tongue in your mouth, guides your hands up under her sweater, and while your hands are thus incarcerated, reaches around and gooses you? Any tips for that scenario?

How about this one: she trudges into your apartment, depressed over some internecine chick skirmish at school, sits down on the floor next to you, expels a lyrical sigh and promptly flops face-first into your crotch.

I'm not finding an entry for *face-first crotch-flopping* in the index of your handbook.

—◻—

When infatuated we experience a surge of dopamine that rushes through the brain causing us to feel good. Irrational romantic sentiments may be caused by oxytocin, a primary sexual arousal hormone that signals orgasm and feelings of emotional attachment. Together these chemicals sometimes override the brain activity that governs logic.
—Relationships counseling website

Okay, okay.

Those emails she sent me when she was a freshman? Enough infatuation to flood the world market and stick it to the damn Ay-rabs.

But these days we no longer even bother with hygienic niceties like shaving, showering, making up. We've seen each other at our respective worsts—have heard, felt, smelled and tasted each other that way, too.

I think it's fairly safe to say that Infatuation has left the building. Infatuation caught the Empire Builder for Wichita, and it's not coming back. *This is no infatuation!* I say, in the snippy tone of young Richard Dreyfuss in *Jaws* declaiming *This was no boating accident!*

No, this is a real monster. It's going to take a big-ass oxygen tank, a harpoon gun and a far more inspiring action hero than Roy Scheider to blow this thing out of the water.

HOW TO PICK UP JAPANESE CHICKS

—◻—

In late autumn, we host more dinner parties for "the kids."

About six chicks are here, bloated and exhausted after a feast of white stew, French bread and three bottles of wine. Chicks this stuffed are so happy, for the moment they don't even care who's demonstrably a virgin and who isn't.

Hiroe's cell rings. It's her boyfriend, out somewhere with Takayuki, the jittery walking smokestack from my remedial class.

Hiroe asks if it's all right to invite them over. I slur some improbable threat to reclaim the ten points that Takayuki swindled from me in a pound of flesh.

"This is serious," the Princess admonishes. "Takayuki stays in his apartment all the time these days. He keeps talking about killing himself."

He has famously attempted suicide once before. Wrist-slashing was his alleged technique, yet the storied forearms bear no distinguishing markings.

Hiroe gets off the phone and announces, to my relief, that my hospitality has been declined. Thus, she has to meet the two boys at a coffee shop. Her friend Chikako declares that she'll go as well. Then so does the Princess. The party dissolves into the now familiar frenzy of dishwashing and grousing over the squalid state of my kitchen.

The Princess takes me aside and tells me she'll come back later, once the crisis is resolved.

At the door, she rushes back inside and kisses me in full view of the others. They find the scene benign, even cute.

—◻—

The Princess returns at dawn.

It took them all night to unravel Takayuki's tale of abusive and unfeeling parents.

I listen yet again to the pathetic saga of Takayuki's life and the even more oft-told inventory of the flaws of Hiroe's boyfriend. I listen because it's my job to listen.

Tenuous as my existence may be, I *do* exist.

I *am*, dammit. I *am* The Boyfriend of a Teenager.

—◻—

I decide that we need a project to work on over the winter.

We'll write a book together. It'll be called *How to Pick Up Japanese Chicks*.

It'll be a parody, of course. The college crowd all over Japan will eat it up.

I've already proved I can write funny in Japanese via my online zine. I have just enough vocabulary to express myself, and just little enough to make plenty of risible usage errors. Sort of a Yakov Smirnoff effect.

We'll write by turns, I figure. It'll be just like our daily email exchanges, only for public consumption. First I'll write a short, incisive essay dissecting the thought processes of Japanese chicks. Then she'll counter with a screed revealing that I'm full of crap. She can illustrate it, too. It'll be part "point-counterpoint," part comic book.

It can't miss.

—◻—

I pitch the idea to her on Christmas Eve. She likes it.

I show her the introductory chapter I've written, and she laughs.

Yay! *Banzai!* We now have something that we can work on together while vertical. Something that mayhap could catalyze this doomed, volatile chemistry experiment of ours into some kind of firm and stable and *kenzen* alloy.

Because God forbid that we should ever be out of each other's lives completely.

—¤—

"But *how* does it end?" she says at last.

It was the three hundred fifty-second "We can't go on like this" that did the trick. Where there had always been outright rejection, now there was an impromptu bedroom press conference.

"I don't know."

"Why? Why don't you know?"

"You're always assuming that I have this thing all mapped out," I gripe. "Don't you see that I'm just as lost as you are? This is all new territory for me, too."

"How do you *think* it ends?"

"You dump me."

"Why would I do that?"

"Because I can't dump you. We already tried it that way. I'm just not strong enough. You're tougher than me."

"That's true."

"I'm a big coward."

"Yeah."

This might be a good time to remind her of her constitutional right to express dissent.

"What about the future?" she asks.

"The future? Well… So, you dump me. I'll be in really bad shape for a while. Really pissed off. I won't talk to you."

"Will you stalk me?"

She sounds oddly hopeful. It throws me off my game.

"Uh, no. Sorry. Stalking is a young man's game. I don't think I'm up to it. No, I'll just stay home and cry, I suppose."

I feel her choking up.

"Not forever. But for a while."

"How long?"

"I don't know. Months. I'm guessing six months."
"Then what?"
"Then maybe we can start to talk a little, but it'll still take more time before it feels right."

She softly sobs.

"But you know what? There's going to come a day when you'll invite me to your home. Your family's home, I mean."

No response. I warm to the theme:

"And I'll come there, and I'll dandle your kids on my knees. And if your husband steps out, we'll talk a little about the way we used to carry on together. And oh, how we'll laugh."

For a while, there is only heaving, congested breathing.

"Your knees," she finally rasps, "are too bony for my kids to sit on."

—◻—

Coming of Age Day: the most superfluous of all Japanese holidays. She and all other new twenty-year-olds throughout the land dress up in kimono or formal suits to sit through skin-moldingly dull ceremonies that in some mystic manner transform them into certified grownups.

I do not attend the event, of course, because her family does. Instead I stay home and wrestle with the Paranoia Brothers: The hideously face-tattooed Oh-God-She'll-Dump-You-Soon and his black-hooded tag team partner No-She'll-Cling-To-You-Forever.

She wants to come over so that I can photograph her in traditional costume. I tell her not to come; it's raining, it's too far to go in such unwieldy garb. Why bother?

She calls after the ceremony and reiterates her desire to come over. I veto it. We stop talking for days.

HOW TO PICK UP JAPANESE CHICKS

> *Teaching Point 17: Whenever a Japanese chick wants to come to your place, for God's sake let her. Even if she's wearing garments that can only be removed with surgical scissors, let her.*

—◘—

When her third year of classes begins, she is fretful. She has been accepted into the department's most exclusive two-year seminar in which she will study anthropology with an emphasis on indigenous peoples. Is she really good enough to cut it with the elite of the department?

I pat her on the fanny and tell her to play nice with the other kids. But somehow we both know then and there:

She's become a woman, and *she* will be the one to put away childish things.

—◘—

That annual Saturday morning comes when I have to examine eighty sophomores applying to take part in short-term exchange programs.

The results of the test are due Monday morning. The Princess has deigned to help me with the intensive marking over the weekend.

I am hung over from a delightfully inane party with one of my new freshman classes and thus am already crabby when she turns up at my office an hour late, more bleary-eyed than I am and not at all inclined to work.

She immediately dials a number on my phone. Getting no answer, she tries again ten minutes later. Then ten minutes later.

"Who are you calling?"
"Takayuki."
"For God's sake, why?"

"His friend did something bad."

—◻—

A major storm has blown up in chick geopolitics, and I will have to hear all about it before any work can get done. This is the life I've chosen.

The previous evening, Hiroe's boyfriend propositioned Chikako by phone. Chikako promptly fled to Hiroe's place and ratted him out. Princess Michiko was summoned to form a chick quorum. They had been up all night cementing chick solidarity, helping Hiroe mull her options, and seeking the culprit's whereabouts.

By the time she has conveyed all this to me, it's time yet again to try Takayuki's place—a likely hideout for the varmint, since they are one another's only known associates.

This time, there is an answer.

"Takayuki-kun?... Michiko... Is he—Oh, he is?... What time?... Uh-huh..."

Then suddenly the tone turns brusque, imperious.

"I called you at three in the morning," she says. "Takayuki-kun, why was some girl in your room answering the phone then?"

I am thinking, *That's a really good question*, and then immediately adding, *An even better one is, Why does she care?*

—◻—

"Hiroe's boyfriend has gone over to her place to apologize," she reports. Even an insensitive dolt like me can see that she is frustrated at not being able to call Hiroe at that moment for fear of intruding.

"Why would a guy *do* something like that?"

"You mean, apologize?"

She glares at me.

"Oh, okay. Why did he proposition Chikako? Well, then. How shall I put this?"

"Tell me. I really don't understand guys."

"Chikako is prettier than Hiroe."

"I don't think so."

I explain that her opinion is not relevant. The desire to engage in pseudo-reproductive acts with Chikako is a perfectly natural one, a desire probably shared by ninety percent of the males on campus, including at least one office-having faculty member. The percentage who hold such feelings toward Hiroe, I note, would be significantly lower—and as far as I know, devoid of faculty members.

"That's all it comes down to? What a girl looks like?"

"When they're as cute as Chikako," I say, "it's enough."

"Geez."

We sit side by side in swivel chairs throughout this discussion, in the midst of which she plops one leg across my lap, inviting me to begin stimulating her through her jeans.

"Look, you don't have to worry. Your desirability quotient is higher than Hiroe's, too. He probably would have hit on you instead if you didn't so obviously despise him."

"It just doesn't seem fair."

She is now returning the manual favor. And yet we keep yapping.

"Maybe it was a vile thing that he did," I say, "but we're all the same. We're animals, really. You can't trust any of us."

"Is that so?"

Then an unforeseen jolt of self-restraint courses through me. Something akin to Responsibility digs its spiked boots into the frozen slope of my psyche.

"We're not going to get any work done here," I say. "I'm going to take this stuff home. You can go help Hiroe change Takayuki's diapers or whatever you have to do, and come over later if you want to."

"What? *No!*"

I have broken the spell. I stand and begin to pack my bag. She grabs my wrist.

"I think you should go."

"Muggy-*chaaan*..."

So much for the miracle of self-restraint.

I lay her down on the desk.

She signals her discomfort. I wad up my jacket and use it to protect her head and my new printer from each other.

> *Teaching Point 18: Enjoy consensual desktop sex with a Japanese chick whenever possible. But mind the delicate appliances.*

—◻—

Let's see now:

Girlfriend sent home in semen-stained garment? Check— had notched that one a long time ago.

Steamy late-night phone calls? Check.

Incriminating gifts? Plenty, both ways.

Sex in the workplace? Check.

We had very nearly collected all the Clinton-Lewinsky merit badges. Close, but no cigar.

—◻—

When it's over, she returns to her chair and begins to cry.

"What's the matter?"

"Not here," she sobs. "I didn't want to do it *here*."

"Oh," I say. "Sorry about that."

"You should go home."

"But I don't want to—"

"Just go. Really, just go. Go home and work. I'll be okay."

So regal and imposing is her tone that—in one of those life-imitates-sitcom moments—I actually start to comply before realizing that this is, after all, my office. Anyway, abandoning a hysterical girlfriend is too cowardly an act even by my standards.

"Let's go together," I say. "Let's go to my place and relax."

"If I go there," she says, "I'll never leave."

"And that's bad because…?"

"I have to think of Hiroe."

"Ah. Let's walk down the hill together then. We'll go have coffee and cake, okay?"

—◻—

She commands me to sit in our local patisserie, place her order, and wait for her return.

I am the proverbial putty in her hands to begin with and, like most men, become even more pliable during the hour or so following an exceedingly pyrotechnic desktop orgasm. And one's pliability factor rises geometrically after watching one's best girl go through an intense crying jag.

Put it all together, and I am Gumby.

She returns in fine spirits. Evidently the chick equivalent of the Cuban Missile Crisis has been resolved to everyone's satisfaction. We kick around plans for a movie date on Wednesday. For the weekend, I've had quite enough of her and still have eighty wretched essays clamoring to be perused.

I walk her to the station and wave her through the gate.

We have had our cake and eaten it too.

All is right with the world.

—◻—

Dear Muggy-chan,

We knew that this day would come eventually, and now it has...

Oh shit. I don't like the sound of that...

I probably should write in English, but to make sure there is no misunderstanding, I write in Japanese...

Easy for you to say. Where's the dictionary? I've got a headache already...

Muggy-chan, there's somebody that I like. In fact, I love him very much. He can't seem to bring himself to say "I love you" yet, but it seems to me that he does care for me, too...

What? Who?? It's been weeks since she even brought up any potential candidates. The only male person she's talked about lately is Takayuki, and he's only hypothetically male.

Oh, God, please, no. Not Takayuki...

...So I want to be with him. I couldn't bear to let him fall into some other woman's hands. That's how much I love him...

Shit. It is Takayuki. Shit, shit, shit.

[Five minutes of whomper-jawed, fade-to-black silence]

...Even before I realized my feeling for him, I had known for some time that you and I would have to separate someday...

You knew, because I kept telling you. And telling you. And telling you...

...But Muggy-chan, oh Muggy-chan! You taught me how to love! You taught me the joy of being truly loved!...

Uh-oh, I think I know what's coming next...

...You are the greatest "teacher" in the world for me. I thank you for everything and...

Don't say it... Please, please, don't say it...

...I will still really like you as my best, best, best friend! *Aiiiiiiiiieeeeeeeeee!!*

Bless you for loving me so much. And know that I, too, loved you as the only lover in the world for me!...

You know, except for the "best friend" twaddle, this is really pretty good...

...Others who look at us could never be made to understand our relationship. To them we are an affront to virtue and common sense...

Dammit, who started all that tickling and finger sucking and rectal poking in public places? Hint: Not me...

...Therefore, being with you was my greatest happiness, but at the same time my heaviest burden...

I bet I've got eight or nine of these messages stashed away somewhere, and this is by far the best written of the lot. Hard to believe it's her first time to write one. You'd think she'd been dumping guys right and left all her life. God, I'm proud of her...

...Even now, the thought of losing you weighs heavily on me. I've been crying all the time, and can't eat or sleep. I know I'll be crying all night tonight...

Only tonight?

...But thanks to the love you gave me, I've learned not to fear or doubt love, and I've become the person I am now for that. Thank you.

This means nothing. She'll change her mind tomorrow and write back. Those buckets of ice-water cascading down the spinal column mean nothing—because it's not over, it's not over...

It's not...is it?

It is. She's given me the heave-ho, given't she...

—◻—

An alternative ending, as seen from the rear of the classroom together the preceding January:

Pursued through the streets of New York by the entire US military, Tom Hanks and his mermaid paramour arrive at the pier, where she must dive in to save herself.

At the last minute, she explains to Tom that he could go with her—that somehow by diving into the harbor with him, she could transform him into a water-breathing merman. The catch is that he could never go back to shore. He would have to sacrifice everything—home, career, even John Candy—for True Love.

He can't go through with it. The cruel, arbitrary gap that Nature has wedged between them simply can't be bridged. He urges her to flee alone for her own safety.

Of course, Tom changes his mind at the last minute, plunges in, and fights off the evil Navy frogmen with plucky Daryl Hannah's help.

They swim together toward a shimmering undersea Atlantis while Rita Coolidge moos through an over-arranged ending theme.

LESSON 10

Honor thy father and thy mother

"You cannot see your way."
"I have no 'way,' and therefore want no eyes."

—*King Lear*

There comes a time in every man's life at least once, and I've had plenty of 'em."

—Casey Stengel

Never date a woman whose father calls her Princess.

—Anonymous Internet advice

I am a saloon ruffian in a Technicolor western. I see the wizened, late-model Duke Wayne waddle up to me; see him grab for my shirt; see the big, meaty fist cock back and then roar forward; and yet I dismiss every opportunity to avoid the punch.

And when my teeth clatter down my gullet, it's as if I never saw it coming at all.

—◻—

There is nobody to chew it over with. Even Dr. Phil has abandoned me.

I lie on my futon staring up at the ceiling all night; through most of the day, too, often enough.

I rehearse conversations that we will have. When she calls and says *A*, I'll fire back with *B*. When she emails and says *C*—oh, boy, I just can't wait for her to say *C*; just let her *try* and get away with *C*—I'll cool her jets with a frigid *D*.

But she doesn't call and she doesn't write, so it's all a wasted exercise. I have no contingency plan for silence.

—◻—

Stage 1: Denial

Remember: She's still got a lot of her stuff in the office—notebooks, CDs and such. If she doesn't pick it up, you have an opening to send an oh-so-chilly email to remind her. If she does, be there in person when it happens.

So you camp in the office. And yet the one day you fail to stake out the turf—Sunday, national hangover day—she slips in.

Your week gets off to a rip-roaring start when you open the office door Monday morning and the spare key jangles loose from the mail chute. And all her stuff is gone.

She came all the way to school on a Sunday only for that?

Then you remember: Takayuki's apartment is a short walk from campus.

—▫—

Tick, tick, tick...

If I hadn't been so cheap when I moved in, I would have sprung for a wall clock with a smooth-flowing second hand.

Instead, you have this constant *tick, tick, tick* bearing down on you. My last checkup revealed fifteen percent hearing loss; I'm often asked to turn down audio materials in class because they're playing much louder than I think they are. And yet, at three in the morning this *tick, tick, TICK* is driving you insane...

I can't even keep my pronouns straight any more. Sometimes I'm *I*, sometimes *you*, sometimes *quob*, a spanking new pronoun of my own making.

—▫—

HOW TO PICK UP JAPANESE CHICKS

Quob go to school every day. Quob pretend that everything is perfectly normal. Quob wave to quobbler acquaintances with the usual jaunty, quobbish smile.

Quob go to classes and muddle through, knowing the course material—and quobbler own jokes—by heart now. Quobbler sense the delivery is tinny and artificial, the performance flawed, but quobbler reputation is so well established among students that no one seems to notice.

They do begin to notice the pale tone and gauntness of quobbler cheeks.

—◻—

It's a beautiful noon hour in early May, the azaleas in full bloom all around, and you have just emerged from your class.

About ten yards ahead, you see her in that black dress. *Probably the first time this year it's been warm enough for that flimsy thing*, you idly note. It no longer works its magic, though; she could be a Southern belle on her way to a funeral.

She's walking perpendicularly across your path toward the entrance to Building 4. You slow your pace and look down.

You spend a lot of time staring into the campus pavement these days, filming it with your eyes. You never realized what fine work they did smoothing the brick walkways. Public television should do a documentary.

Though your eye cameras are angled downward, she's still in frame. You sense the moment she notices your approach. Her pace picks up. She's more than flouncing but not quite running. She is *strolling*, gaily and prettily strolling.

What, or who, is she strolling for?

She turns around and gives the *hurry up* sign.

A scrawny, androgynous figure lopes into the frame. *What's the big rush?* He is bemused, taking his time, puffing on his cigarette. She strolls and gestures all the more frantically, trying to usher him out of the shot before you look up.

Too late.

Do not ask for whom the belle strolls.

—◻—

I am a man who once sat in an overpriced hotel room across from the White House glued to my TV set all afternoon, having canceled plans to visit the Smithsonian because a "sexual thriller" starring Annabella Sciorra came on a cable channel, and the odds seemed good of seeing Annabella Sciorra naked before it was over, and in my warped little mind this trumped anything the Smithsonian might have to offer.

The closest thing to a payoff one gets, however, is the climax, in which it turns out that the shadowy figure who has been bedeviling Annabella all along is her kindly old mentor Alan Alda, who chases her out of the house and into the dark, foamy ocean until somehow she comes up with a spear gun with which she shoots him in the forehead.

Alan Alda did not handle this scene well. An old *M*A*S*H* fan myself, I am loath to admit that his death-rasps[*] will not be enshrined alongside those of *The Godfather*'s Sterling Hayden and *Alien*'s John Hurt in the Death Rasp Hall of Fame anytime soon.

But then, I am a man who would ask Alan Alda's detractors, "How does an actor prepare for a scene in which his character is unexpectedly—or expectedly, for that matter—shot in the forehead with a spear gun by a soggy B-movie actress?"

What sort of life experience is one supposed to draw on for that?

Thought I was pretty sassy when that question first popped into my mind. But now I think I know the answer.

I am a man who now knows exactly how a spear through the forehead feels.

---

[*] Roughly *"Awwk…Awwk…Awwk…"*

Stage 2: Temporary Insanity
Tick, tick, tick...

The apocryphal deathbed words of Oscar Wilde, an esthete to the end, were "Either those drapes go, or I do."

I'm thinking, "Either that clock battery expires, or I do."

—□—

I would have gone mad much sooner than I did if not for classes.

Room 214 became my cocoon, a familiar and cozy sanctuary where business went on as usual. No strolling, liberated Princesses could assail me here. I could run through my usual shtick and the students would love it, just as their predecessors in Room 214 had for going on ten years. When my eyes watered, surely they chalked it up to late-spring allergies.

But 214 looks out on a pathway that students from off-campus housing use when walking to school, and more than once I would see Takayuki saunter by.

Few students in the history of our department had become more justly famed for not coming to school. Now I was seeing him bound eagerly up the path.

Twice a day sometimes.

That was odder still, but not inexplicable. He lived so close to school that he might go home for lunch.

Later, I started seeing him come up the path three, five, ten times a day. Eventually every third biped life form traipsing by the window was another Takayuki. Sometimes I envisioned an enormous bald eagle swooping down to devour him.

I tried to imagine what the vomited pellet of his undigested remains would look like, and cackled aloud at the thought, alarming the freshmen.

That's when I first knew I was in trouble.

—◘—

One unit of our first-year syllabus centered on the language function of describing personalities and interests. As a supplement, I photocopied a page of mug shots of famous celebrities—sumo wrestlers, hot comedians, and of course myself—for distribution in class.

"Suppose that you don't know these people," I said. "Just create their personality from your impression of the faces, using English words."

Year after year my picture had elicited predictable comments:

He's a heavy drinker.
He's funny.
He might be gay.
His hobby is making music.
He must like underage girls.
He has a large adult video collection.
He is very cheerful.
He is too cheerful.
He is dangerous.

This year, the comments took on a different hue:
He is sad.
He has no friends.
His hobby is looking at the ground.
He is deeply neurotic.
He must live alone, because no one wants to live with him.

—◘—

One day, shaving my head in front of the bathroom mirror, I heard a voice say, *Where is it written that you have to have that gray beard?*

I hacked it off. My lower face saw daylight for the first time since the Carter administration.

"You look…younger!" I was often told. *Surely they mean better, more virile, sexier*, the voice assured.

Why stop at the neck? the voice—it may have been the clock, for lack of other suspects—advised.

And so I de-furred myself, clearing away old-growth chest foliage.

Oh, what the hell. Go for the porn star look.

I did finally stop around the knees.

—◻—

After the defoliation, I could see some of the other changes.

My ribs were showing through the skin.

And as a little more time passed, they were visible through my shirts. They were clearly defined, countable.

In my line of work, I'm paid to know and explain the difference between a countable and an uncountable noun, so I know whereof I speak. These ribs were most definitely countable.

Former students who had gone abroad for the one-year exchange program began trickling back in late May and early June, and recoiled like Camp Crystal Lake counselors at the sight of me.

I had not achieved the porn star look. I had instead achieved the forty-five-year-old adolescent going through chemotherapy look.

The two are quite different.

—◻—

You continue to have these debates with the invisible Princess. I mean, *I* have debates with her. Or maybe *quob* does. It doesn't matter.

The Princess is always there, and she says E and I answer F. And she says G and I retort *Don't give me that G shit. H! Yeah, you heard me! H, baby! Take that!.*

And then right in the middle of this alphabet game some internal buzzer sounds the end of the period, and like a Zamboni the crying machine rolls onto the ice and merrily fills up the down time.

—◻—

Instead of H, perhaps I'll tell her about seeing Takayuki pull up to our neighborhood convenience store on his scooter with a non-Princess chick clinging to his waist.

He peels her off his torso long enough to pump some coins into the cigarette machine—allowance from those cruel parents back home, no doubt, since his disabilities preclude him from holding a job—and then casually putt-putts away, looking no more beset by inner demons than Mister Rogers.

I'm pretty sure this is real.

—◻—

Introducing the foolproof West Yokohama Diet!

Breakfast: Aspirin and coffee
Lunch: Water
Dinner: A convenience store salad; water
Before bed: Wine (one bottle);
over-the-counter sleeping pills (two);
cough syrup (as needed)

Never again feel ashamed of your love handles!

HOW TO PICK UP JAPANESE CHICKS

Never again feel rejected and doomed!
Never again feel, period.

—▫—

I'm sitting in my office one day and I realize that I have Takayuki's home phone number on file from his stint as my quasi-student the year before.

I call it on impulse. Would he answer his phone? Would *she*? Somebody else? Oh, let it be an unfamiliar female voice...

It is a very familiar female voice. Not hers, though. It is the same robotic chick who drones the leave-your-message spiel on my own machine.

—▫—

It is my custom to write the list of the day's activities on the board before a lesson starts so that students can visualize the ninety-minute pedagogical miracle that is to follow, thusly:

No Quiz today
Kenji's presentation
Review of movie Scene 14
Movie Scene 15
Return of previous Quiz
Announcements

At the end of one lesson in May, I will turn to the board and find, to my bewilderment, the following:

No Quiz today
No Presentations
No, nothing like that today.
Just the same, old crap.
The same thing as yesterday, the same as tomorrow

and tomorrow, and tomorrow…
…Creeps in this petty pace from day to day till the last syllable of recorded time.
It is a lesson taught by an idiot!
Nothing ever changes.
I hate this job.
I hate this life.

After the bell, a quiet lad will pause on his way out the door to inquire after his teacher's health.

— ▫ —

It's around this time that I begin to notice another peculiar thing: Somebody has been using my skin.

I don't know who it is. It could be an alien body snatcher, or a minion of the damned. Perhaps it's the recently disincarnated spirit of Sir John Gielgud. That would be nice. I liked him in *Arthur*.

Whatever. This entity is waking up with the alarm every morning and trudging off to school. It is teaching my classes for me. It's using my textbooks, it's giving my assignments, it's telling my jokes.

It makes exactly the same snide crack about the picture of the spooky looking white guy on page forty-eight of the textbook that I have made for a decade, even though I'm now spookier-looking than he.

I can't say that the entity meets my standards. It has fallen more than a week behind my pace covering the material and yet doesn't seem to mind, and it's often a half-beat off with the timing of punch lines.

Still, I suppose I should be grateful, since its efforts keep the salary flowing into my bank account month after month, allowing me to buy more wine, more sleeping aids, more cough syrup.

Isn't that just the darnedest thing, though? Don't you just hate it when an entity takes over your skin?

—☐—

At times it seems natural, in a way. After all, I have this perfectly serviceable forty-five-year-old skin, with much less wear and tear than most skins of that vintage. And I'm certainly not doing anything with it. So why not let somebody else sit at the wheel, take 'er out and put 'er through 'er paces?

And if I met the entity that borrows my skin, I would have to tell it that I like the upgrades.

Hey, I would say, *Love what you've done with the exterior. You know, getting rid of that awful old gray beard, ditching the love handles and then some. I don't think the muscle tone has ever been this good.*

So there is much to be thankful for. Still, I am wary of the entity's continued presence, lest it settle in and get too cozy. If it gets caught pulling some of its antics, ignorant witnesses are likely to blame poor innocent me.

And some of the things it does are awful, just unspeakable. If I were doing them, I could never forgive myself. So I thank God it's not me, but still it's damned awkward sitting here in this dreamy, doped-up carcass, getting led around by the nose, seeing all these terrible events unfold...

It calls Takayuki all the time now, for one thing. And I mean all the time.

At least it has the common sense not to do this from my apartment so that nothing can be traced back here. It uses various pay phones in the area, and has probably gone through thousands in ten-yen calls.

Sometimes it hangs up as soon as Takayuki, or whoever, answers. After a while, Takayuki refuses to answer, starts screening with the answering machine. And my entity leaves a long silent message at the beep—as much eerie nothingness as ten yen will buy.

Now and again it'll spring for twenty yen of air time.

Sometimes I get up in the morning (or afternoon on weekends) and notice mud on my shoes, and then I know that something not of this world has been abroad that night.

After a while, though, all that seems…quite all right.

—◻—

Dante got it right. If you're going to do the Paradise-Hell-Purgatory grand tour, you should get the nasty stuff out of the way early and save the best for last. I wish somebody had reminded me of that before I started out.

—◻—

Stage 3: Temporary Sanity

The voice on the other end is male, British, calm, professional, effeminately soft.

"How long have you been thinking that you might kill yourself?"

"It's been about a month now."

"And what was the incident that made you begin to think this way? A problem in a relationship perhaps?"

This guy is *good*.

"Yes. A relationship ended suddenly."

"That's rough."

"Yes."

"Please understand that I have to ask these questions."

"It's okay."

"Have you already decided on a method?"

The tone is as benign as *Can I get you an appetizer?*

"Yes. Hanging."

"Have you bought the rope yet?"

Whoa. What a waste of talent. He ought to be playing the MGM Grand with this routine.

"I was thinking of an extension cord. I have a good, strong one."

"And the place?"

"Here. In my private office at school, I mean."

"Why there?"

"It's indoors, and I'd be found fairly soon."

The janitor here has always given me the creeps, so I figure turnabout is fair play.

—¤—

Pamela will be my therapist this evening. She, too, is a one-name artist. The setting is a musty study in a church in the Motomachi district.

What makes you feel like hurting yourself?… Uh-huh… And how do you feel about this girl now?… What makes you say that?… Do you care so much about what other people think of you?… Why?…

I'm thinking all this Socratic hack-your-own-way-out-of-the-jungle rubbish is just the warm-up, but it turns out to be the whole workout. The three one-hour sessions that I manage to drag myself through yield not one crumb of useful advice and but three thought-provoking words.

They come when I am lured into giving a long, rambling inventory of the things I miss about the Princess, which is easy enough to do—by this point, I even miss the irksome finger in my rectum, though I do not share this with Pamela—and when I come to the scent of her hair I choke up, and that's when she says:

"You are mourning."

—¤—

There's a moment in the science fiction movie *Cocoon*—another Ron Howard opus that I had used in class—in which one of the titular cocoons is opened to reveal a dying alien inside.

He's a pruny, Bambi-eyed specter. The soundtrack swells so poignantly that one really feels for Brian Dennehy, the leader of the alien landing party, as his eyes overflow and he marvels at this unfamiliar emission.

"I never knew anyone who died before," he says.

Hey, same here.

So I was mourning. This is what it tasted like. And this is what the great romance of my life had finally withered away to:

A dead raisin from space.

—◻—

Only one thing changed. Raisins joined the long list of things the sight of which made me weep, joining:
1. Video rental boxes for any movie we had seen together
2. My own office, and in particular the vacant desk in my office
3. Advertisements featuring smiling young women in bras
4. A return to or passing by of any shop that we had browsed in, restaurant or café that we had been served in, open space that we had lolled in, or street that we had walked down.

To visit my therapist, I had to de-train at Ishikawa-cho Station and walk past the very bench where she and I had canoodled that summer day when outed by Wakako.

It was unbearable to see the disrespectful way people milled around it—even sat on it—as if it were an ordinary bench. It should have been glassed off, like the Shroud of Turin or the window of the Texas Book Depository.

So much for talk therapy.

—◻—

Minding my own business one morning, tuned into oldies radio, I am assaulted by "The End of the World."

For perhaps the three hundredth time in my life, I hear the familiar pleas for enlightenment as to why those birds go on singing, why the stars glow above, etc. After all, the song concludes, the world ended when I lost your love.

Once, overhearing an earnest young English teacher's deconstruction of these very words, I marveled at their banality. Now the scales fall from my eyes.

My God, that's brilliant! It's absolute genius!

I finally got it.

—¤—

My last stab at therapy yielded this memorable exchange:

"Maybe we should examine what sort of support network you have."

"What," I asked, "is a support network?"

"Well, your friends and family," she said. "All the people who might come to your aid in a time of need make up what we call a support network."

"Oh, that," I said. "I don't got me one of those."

—¤—

Or did I?

A secretary in our department's office with whom I had seldom exchanged more than passing pleasantries began foisting homemade lunches on me. I would take a few polite nibbles for her, then abscond to some place where she could not see me throw the rest away.

Kindness, or even pity, if that's what it was, was welcome. Food, I still believed, was overrated.

—¤—

Next up to the plate was Professor Twain.

He came by my office, took a seat, and eyed the thick extension cord on my desk with puzzlement.

His first order of business was to confirm the rumor that he had, indeed, been offered a position at an Ivy League school and would be returning to the Great Satan at the end of the spring semester. The yammering nincompoop Professor Tachibana would be his successor as supervisor of my program. This would have been horrible news had I thought that I myself would still be around to work with her.

Then this followed.

"There's a lot of concern about you in the department," he said. "You don't seem to be yourself these days."

"I've felt better. But I haven't missed a class day."

"Nobody's worried about your job performance. It's about you."

Now he'd done it. Whatever prostate-like organ is responsible for churning out tears kicked into high gear, and I had to pour all my energies into staving off an ocular orgasm.

Grandma naked! Grandma naked! I chanted internally. It had always been my best bet for staving off premature emissions at the other end, and darned if it didn't work just as well on the tear ducts.

He leaned forward and with a subtle shift of tone magically metamorphosed from Professor Twain, supervisor, into plain old Randall.

"If there's something you want to tell me," he said, "I promise it won't leave this room."

"Ah...ah...," I said, as if testing a mike. Satisfied that my voice was free of quaver, I proceeded: "I've been told that I'm suffering from acute depression."

"I see," he said. "Told by whom?"

"I've been in touch with that hotline service for foreign residents," I said, "and they referred me to a network of counselors. I've been seeing this American woman."

"Are you taking anything for it?"

"Bron cough syrup."

"I mean real prescribed medications."

"I hear they wouldn't be covered by health insurance," I said. "Neither is the counseling, since she's not licensed."

"Is it Catherine DeLozier that you're seeing?" he said.

"No, I don't know that name."

"She's the person in charge of that whole outfit."

"You know a lot about this."

He reached into his bag, giving me hope that I could watch him shoot up again. He was diabetic and had once let me see him self-medicate in his office. But he simply took out a cloth for wiping his glasses.

"I went through a rough patch with my wife a few years ago," he said. "We did counseling together."

"I see."

"The rest of the family never felt comfortable in Japan." I noticed he was already using past tense. An English teacher picks up on these things. "Our son got mixed up with drugs, got picked up once. My wife felt that I was concentrating on work and neglecting the family."

I had been dimly aware that Randall was married, but had not known he had a son old enough to commit felonies.

"Our boy's doing okay now," he went on. "He's in college in California. My wife and I are still struggling to work things out, though."

"Ah."

"The point is, just don't think you're the only one with troubles. As they say, there comes a time in every man's life."

He took another, longer glance at the cord that lay cobra-like on my desk as he rose.

"I don't think you realize what an asset you are to this university. We certainly don't want to lose you."

—◻—

And there it was. That was the instant that I became a sympathy junkie.

The first sample is always free. The rest you have to work for.

—◻—

Stage 4: Adaptation
"Hi, Muggins! Hey, are you okay?"
"I'm depressed. Intermittently suicidal."
"Whoa, that sucks. Anything we can do for you? Cook? Clean your house? Flash our breasts?"

My real interactions with NU chicks are not yet this crude, but we can work on that.

—◻—

Bat Girl, a/k/a Nozomi, calls.
"Muggins! Did you eat anything tonight?"
"No. No. I just didn't feel like it."
"Well, hang on! I'm coming over!"

Nozomi has taken it upon herself to nursemaid me, much as some adoring fan did for Samuel Clemens in his declining years.

She arrives by motor scooter minutes later to rescue me with microwaved dishes from Seven Eleven. I call her Bat Girl. I have told her I am going to make a bat-symbol searchlight that I can project on night clouds over our neighborhood to summon her.

I don't think she gets the reference, but she laughs heartily. She laughs heartily at pretty much anything. If she were older, whiter, maler and a lot lumpier, she'd make an ideal talk-show sidekick.

I tell her that her presence gives me a better appetite, and I'm not kidding. She laughs anyway.

—◻—

She is nervous because she is a senior and her job search is going nowhere. Most of her classmates have already secured promises of postgraduate employment.

She is aiming for flight attendant or, failing that, a position at a major hotel. English interviews are part of the recruitment process for either job, so she asks me to help her practice. I do. By now I have a two-decade history of getting chicks into flight attendant jobs.

Between rehearsals she asks, "So what happened to you, anyway?"

And I tell her the story.

More accurately, I tell her *a* story. Like an effective résumé, my version of the story highlights the favorable truths—my frequent encouragements to the Princess to find someone her own age, my gracious bowing out when she finally did—while casually omitting unpleasant ones, such as the alien entity that nocturnally seizes control of my skin.

Bat Girl listens, enraptured, and does not laugh.

> *Teaching Point 19: Chicks love few things more than the tale of someone else's doomed love affair.*

There is a pregnant pause during which I dare to hope that she might try to rape me. Instead, she reciprocates by telling me her own doomed-love-affair story.

In her last year of high school, she attended a cram school to prepare for college entrance exams. A chubby Japanese teacher of English had charmed her. She was seventeen, he was forty-one. They have been lovers ever since.

"What do you do for a good time with him?" I ask.

"He's busy, so we only meet on weekends."

"You go to movies? Go out to dinner?"

"No, hardly ever. He doesn't have much money. He still lives with his parents and he's saving for a place of his own."

"You don't go out for drinks? Go to the beach? Go to Tokyo Disneyland? Stuff like that?"

"No, never."

"What *do* you do, then?"

"He comes over on Sundays, and I cook for him."

"And you never go out?"

"He takes me to flea markets."

"Excuse me, did you say *flea markets*?"

"He collects CDs. He has thousands of them. He gets used ones on sale at flea markets."

"What a fun guy!"

She laughs, but without the usual gusto.

"Do you love him?"

"I don't know. I think I do."

"Why do you *think* so?"

"He brings his shirts with him when he comes down on Sundays, and I iron them."

As my jaw detaches from my skull she adds, "Well, I wouldn't do that if I didn't love him, would I?"

The Story has real potential. I rehearse and polish it till I can deliver it as smoothly as the latest news from Lake Wobegon.

A six-pack of sophomore girls comes for a sleepover to cheer me up. I clobber them with The Story. Some are in tears.

But again, nobody rapes me. Six of them, after all. It's too crowded for that. Note for future (if any) reference: Thin out their numbers.

—◻—

Word of my sympathy jones is getting around. All around the world, it seems.

My sister calls, followed by my brother, both asking what's up and telling of turmoil in their families that I had never suspected.

A woman named Erika from the previous year's TOEFL class drops by my office to hear The Story and to share hers.

She's twenty-six, ancient by Japanese college standards. She had to quit an office job after a torrid affair with her married supervisor. So she decided to come back to school after a year and a half of total immobility in her room.

My God, people sure are effed up.

—◻—

Now I am dating Erika. Bat Girl is coming over often and sometimes we go out for drinks. A double dose of college chicks, one would think, would suffice to snap a depressed middle-aged English teacher out of it.

But in fact, nothing is going on.

Bat Girl certainly has the face and figure of a future flight attendant. But I've never been a flight attendant kind of guy. I make a heroic effort to masturbate to her but she fails the audition. I don't have the heart to tell her.

Erika, being more Rubenesque, tends to perform better in Fantasy Theater. Real life, however, is inconveniently real.

She permits hand-holding and, when out of public view, short kisses.

But she is still hurting from her own debacle and I, despite having heard nothing from Dr. Phil in months, detect a tiny cache of residual conscience radiating somewhere in the attic of my psyche, so I do not press the matter.

Still, all this mercy dating just is not cutting it any more. My sympathy jones is growing by the day. I crave bigger doses.

— ◻ —

If only I could approach strangers on the street and offer them oral sex in exchange for sympathy. Unfortunately, the time-honored tactics of the conventional junkie are not open to me.

I will have to cast the net wider, and I have just the tool to do it: my website.

In early spring, I had completed a new edition of my online zine, with a new interview in my Great Women of NU series (featuring Wakako, oddly enough—my adversary in the Ishikawa-cho Station incident). Thus, I am still projecting my jolly old eccentric and contented self to the outside world. That just won't do.

I take the whole website down.

Next I take my own picture. Several of them. Indeed, I put myself through a whole Maxim shoot:

Come on, baby, show us a little desiccation… No, no, the sad-clown face looks forced… Not so blank, baby… It's sympathy we want here, remember?... Yeah! The wistful smile! Tell the world how your life has turned to gorilla-shit stew! Oh, yeah, baby! The wistful smile! You'll have them pounding down your door!

I post the winning wistful-smile-because-my-life-has-turned-to-gorilla-shit-stew shot above a brief message saying that my website is suspended indefinitely for health reasons. With a handy email link.

It occurs to me frequently during these processes that this is the most juvenile thing I've done in at least two decades. It doesn't stop me. For years this site has been averaging over ten hits a day. But who are these people? Only one way to find out.

I upload. I sit back. I wait.

I guess this is what ice-fishing must be like.

—◻—

One of the first nibbles is from an alumna named Mayumi. She graduated three years ago. I can barely remember what she looked like.

Now she writes:

You have no right to take down that website. I'm sorry that you're not in good condition, but I need that website. College was the only happy time of my life, and that website was the only way I had of making it come alive again. It picks me up when I need picking up. I need it a lot.

Don't you dare leave it down.

Yes, indeed—everybody's life is plenty effed up.

—◻—

Ayana chimes in for the first time in over a year. She is in Southeast Asia on a research grant.

What the hell's wrong with you? she asks, and I write out The Story for her.

Let me get this straight, she fires back. *You weren't just hanging out with this chick the way you and I used to. You were actually having sex with her?*

I picture the nose-crinkling, upper-teeth-baring disgust with which she typed the last five words.

I doubt there is any sympathy to be milked from Ayana, but I nonetheless press on with a more detailed account, even unto the fabled Ferris wheel ride.

Look, she responds. *You had a good time with this girl. It's over. Enjoy the memory of it from time to time, but move on. Jesus.*

—◻—

She is the only person giving me my medicine straight. Everything she says rings true. I begin to see her as some kind of virgin-savant.

Still, she isn't seeing the whole picture. I try again, this time including excerpts from my email exchanges with the Princess, including that expertly crafted Dear John message.

Is this chick some kind of fucking moron, or what?

—◻—

I accuse Ayana of callousness. No, I say, the Princess is *not* a moron, as should be evidenced by the fact that I loved her—and still do. And anyway, who was Ayana to be passing judgment? What did she know about this kind of pain?

Okay, okay, I get it now, she replies. And then, like all the others, she launches into her own tales of woe.

In the countless hours of our many outings that long-ago summer, I thought we had drunk our way through her entire inventory of miseries. It turns out that there is a whole cellarful of vintage pain that she reserves for special occasions. I am now allowed a few samples, which I consume with astonishment.

Ayana, I write back, *you know what? Everybody is effed up! All these people who seemed to lead perfectly contented lives—don't! Every single human being is totally effed up!*

Two days later she replies: *You're forty-something, and you're just figuring that out* now?

HOW TO PICK UP JAPANESE CHICKS

—◻—

Further down the Jeopardy category of "Chicks Deemed Morons by Ayana" were her own erstwhile classmates Hanae and Yuri, whose qualifications as strippers had once been a topic of animated discussion. On cue, Hanae emails me the next day to voice concern about the horrid picture on the website.

She insists on coming over that Saturday. And since she lives way out in suburban Chiba, she figures she'd better plan on staying the night. Moreover, she will look into enlisting Yuri and another friend, Naomi.

Three chicks with boobs as big as their heads, I think. Then, a minute later, for my brain is churning ever more slowly from the daily infusions of alcohol and cough syrup…

That's six boobs!

—◻—

Actually, only four.

Naomi's couldn't make it. In fact, Naomi and her breasts didn't make it anywhere these days. Once the ripest tomato of her bumper-crop frosh class, she has fallen into such a deep funk that she cannot leave the family home.

Good lord…

Even so, the combined presence of Hanae, still in possession of Japan's largest collection of snug, low-cut tops, and the delightfully earthy Yuri grants me a remission.

They drink heavily. They reminisce about school days. I achieve invisibility for stretches of time, during which I catch up on my own drinking and perve on their cleavage.

Finally, Yuri says, "So what the hell is wrong with you, anyway?"

I tell them The Story.

—◘—

A vaudeville performer once made a career for himself out of reciting *Casey at the Bat* night after night to thousands of audiences, never failing to rev himself up for the big climax and then break down in tears at the tragic ending. I have my drill down, too.

Like all oft-told tales, mine gets stretched, creased and scrunched in places with the constant retelling. More and more is made of my heroic restraint upon getting the boot.

"I have not spoken to her nor tried to make contact with her since that day," I conclude, voice cracking. "Every time the phone rings, I expect it to be her. But it never is, and there's nothing I can do about it. I—I have to leave her alone to grow up to be the great lady that I expect her to be."

"You've never told her how bad you feel without her?"

"No, *no!* No, I don't dare."

"Dare!" they implore. *"Dare!"*

—◘—

Hanae cries. Yuri, not the crying type, smokes.

At least, she tries to smoke, but is not permitted. It is my place and I don't care, but Hanae does, and she makes Yuri go outside.

Showers are taken. I keep drinking until I realize that nobody is going to go to bed unless I suggest it. So I excuse myself and crawl into the bedroom.

Hanae follows. Yuri stays in the living room. She has a TV show she always watches on Saturday nights.

In the dark, I ask Hanae to tell me her own life-is-effed-up story, and she does.

Her story does not leave a memory imprint, partly because all these tales of woe are starting to run together, and partly because my brain is overheating from the flood of data being transmitted through the fingers of my right hand, which Hanae has allowed to manipulate her left breast.

Being regarded as harmlessly insane, I have figured out, is about the best thing that can happen to a middle-aged man in Japan. It is better than being invisible.

—◻︎—

Predawn light seeps into the bedroom as my hands overflow with Yuri's breasts. Not Hanae's. Yuri's.

How did that happen? Maybe we were both dreaming of long-lost lovers. Maybe I was having a nightmare about fending off two humongous jellyfish.

What does it matter? These are breasts that I once admired from a fifth-floor vantage point, breasts that I have been yearning to see since the salad days of Dan Quayle, breasts that once lasted sixty-three weeks on the Fantasy Top Forty and still get loads of airplay on the oldies station.

I am awake enough now to peer over Yuri's mountain range and determine that Hanae is breathing deeply, facing toward the wall, perhaps even awaiting her turn. Did the Make-a-Wish Foundation set this up? You *guys!*

Yuri raises a finger to her lips to signal the need for quiet. Since this is so faithfully following a fantasy screenplay I optioned years ago, and since her hands, unlike mine, are unoccupied, I begin to direct one toward gainful employment.

And then the phone rings.

—◻︎—

"Answer it," Yuri whispers. "It might be *her.*"

Her who?

Oh, yeah.

And mightn't it be? After all, who calls at six on Sunday morning? Might it not be a desperate former lover fleeing a date-rapist with no place left to turn?

I stagger up. My frustrated little friend invades living room airspace and the rest of me follows a phone-ring later.

"*Moshi-moshi*," I say.

"*Ohio!*" booms a voice. It is not the Princess. It is not female. It is a voice that, under the circumstances is hard to place, yet at the same time is one of the most familiar of all.

"Good morning!" chimes in another.

"Dad! Mom!"

"Hi! Is it too early? What time is it there?"

"Ahh… Ohh…" *The big hand says it's quarter past two chicks in the sack, Mom.*

"Guess we woke you up, huh?"

"No. I was…up."

By now, the big hand is no longer so big.

"Is everything all right?"

Behind me the front door opens as Yuri steps outside to smoke.

"Everything's fine here. Just fine."

"We heard you were sad about something."

"I'm *fine!*"

—¤—

That's my sleeping-with-two-chicks story. Not much by NBA standards, to be sure. But at least I have one; so there.

I've fondled three breasts of former students in one night. Not a lot, I know—if you wadded them all up in a ball, you could still shoot a free throw and get nothing but net—but I'm confident it places me in the all-time top five for faculty members at our century-old university, it being a Christian institution and all. Sometimes I feel that it's an omission not to include this on my curriculum vitae.

HOW TO PICK UP JAPANESE CHICKS

The trouble with having a sleeping-with-two-chicks story to tell—pathetic though it might be—is that it crosses one more item off the shrinking list of Things To Do Before You Die.

LESSON 11

Or Stage Five—
The Moment of Clarity

It's easy for men with immature personalities to develop addictions to women. Their bonds with their mothers are excessively strong.

—Japanese sociology journal article quoted in a chat room for expats

This seems to fit the description of the loser gaijin, who hardly got laid at home and then starts going crazy in Japan.

—Anonymous chat participant

When choices need to be made, I surprise myself by making the life-affirming one.

Newsweek sends me an expiration notice. I renew.

My local hospital reminds me of our standing date for a midsummer colonoscopy, and who can say no to that?

—◻—

Pamela calls to ask why I have not scheduled another session. I lie that I'm getting medication, and can't afford the costs of both meds and counseling.

The legendary Catherine DeLozier, doyenne of counseling for the English-speaking community in Japan, calls a few days later with the same question.

"Are you sure there isn't a problem with Pamela?" she asks.

"What do you mean?"

"If it's the quality of the counseling, we can provide a replacement."

"No," I assure her. "Pamela is doing her best."

That sounds weak. I grope for a better endorsement that won't ring false. "Pamela is a good listener."

—◻—

What I need is a talker.

I need a tall penile-domed Texan to kick my ass around the saloon a few times and tell me that by God, what I need to do is to clean up my act, by God, while his gap-toothed studio audience hoots and hollers.

Damn, I miss Dr. Phil.

—¤—

Pamela herself calls again a few days later.

"If there's something about the sessions that you don't like, we can make changes," she whines.

"No, no. Why would you say that?"

"Catherine called me after you talked to her the other day. I gather that you're not happy with my work."

"No. Like I told her, it's just a matter of money."

She hesitates. "I'm no longer associated with…" and names the counseling organization that Catherine heads. "If you'd like to continue the sessions, we could negotiate a new rate just between us."

Wonderful. I'm the hot Free Agent of the Therapy League off-season.

—¤—

The messages of concern or objection in response to the quasi-shutdown of my website keep coming in. I lose count at seventy. Alumni not sighted in years raise their periscopes.

It's just like the last act of *It's a Wonderful Life*, except no quirky angel will trick me into saving myself and I will go to Hell.

Otherwise, quite the same.

—¤—

The translucent-skinned elves of the NU accounting office fire off a fax composed in almost impenetrable grovel-ese. Seems they've been underpaying me for the past two years, and would I mind very much if they deposited the equivalent of twenty thousand dollars in my bank account?

I take Erika to the most expensive restaurant I can find.

I take Bat Girl to Tokyo Disneyland, where her cheap-ass, flea-market-surfing boyfriend has never taken her.

I even take Yuri out on a date once. I figure that she's far too fine a lady to allow herself to be felt up in bed by some old creep she has never dated, even if the order of events is a bit off kilter. We have a pleasant if smoky dinner during which she finally tells me *her* my-life-is-effed-up stories, of which she has two packs worth.

I update Ayana on my antics and bounce the idea off her of blowing the remainder of my windfall on sex tourism in Thailand.

She reminds me that Thai prostitutes are sold into sexual slavery, often in childhood, and suggests I need somebody to ream me out so I know how it feels to be violated.

—◻—

It's beautiful in there, I think, idly, dopily. *No wonder the Princess loved to go poking around.*

On the monitor the washed-out intestinal canal appears pink and clean and seemingly endless. At the end of it, one expects the camera to encounter a white light and the Archangel Gabriel.

Just then, something wicked our way comes: an unsightly clump of tissue that just doesn't belong in Rectal Paradise. It has ridges—roundish purple layers that rise and fall along the surface. It looks as though the Michelin Man has lain down for a nap smack in the middle of my bowel.

There is the insertion of cutting implements. Rivulets of blood squirt out and float weightless. A slight internal twinge accompanies each slice and cut, but nothing more. It is a blurry outtake from a Tarantino film, something happening far away.

It is a long scene; Quentin would never permit such senseless repetition

—◻—

"It's not like last year's polyp," the proctologist says, harkening back the fond memory of an endearing little fella that was easily lassoed and excised, and bless its heart later found to be utterly benign. "This one's bigger—much bigger. But it's low-lying so we can't cut it out with instruments."

"So, what do we do?"

"We'll biopsy the tissue that I excised today," he says.

"How does it look, though?"

"I can't say." But his face speaks volumes.

—◻—

Upon arriving home, I settle down to contemplate slow death from colon cancer while simultaneously indulging in my new hobby: listening to the clock on the wall...*tick, tick, tick.*

They keep promising us a big killer earthquake. It's been nearly seventy years since the last one, and they keep saying we're overdue. Wouldn't this be a lovely time to have it? Collapse the building, send me plummeting down to the first floor... Let a nice, friendly concrete slab put me and that clattering clock and Michelin Man—the whole lot of us—out of our misery...

Nothing I hate more than promises not kept. If I could figure out where "they" were, those lying sacks of seismological shit, by God, I would give them a piece of my mind. And a piece of my colon, too, for good measure.

The phone. It might have been ringing for hours.

"This is Kazuyo."

"*Who* is Kazuyo?"

This stumps her.

"*This* is. Um, *Kazuyo*... Kazuyo from English class?"

"Oh. Hi, Kazuyo."

"What are you doing now?"

I'm not sure how to express *Wishing for a concrete slab to crush me beyond recognition* in Japanese, so I say nothing.

"Well," she continues, "remember Yoro-no-taki, the place we partied at before? We're all here now 'cause a lot of us go back to our hometowns tomorrow for the summer. Wanna come have a drink?"

"Sure."

―◻︎―

By late afternoon the next day my drugstream has been sufficiently polluted with red blood cells as to allow me to rise from my futon.

I send the customary post-party emails: One to Kazuyo to disavow responsibility for anything I may have said or done in the hours prior to waking up in her apartment at three a.m.; and one to a girl named Mai to apologize for hitting on her, vaguely hoping that she'll write back and say no, no, that's all right and that she really does want to spend a romantic scuba-diving weekend in Okinawa with me.

But she has gone back to her provincial hometown and probably will not check her school mail account till September. So there is no reply. There is only the ticking of the damn clock.

For five hours there was painless, fulfilling joy. For twelve subsequent hours, there was painless oblivion. Then I woke up, and promptly vowed never to repeat this mistake.

Waking up, that is.

—¤—

Day and night bleed together. The clock keeps on ticking.

—¤—

The clock, at some point, stops ticking and starts talking.

It's a beautiful Saturday, it says.

"Yes, I know," I reply. "I hate beautiful Saturdays."

You always imagine her out on a date with somebody else.

"You know it."

Go out and find a hooker. You can always pretend it's her.

"No. I've had it with sex. Sex is overrated."

Yeah.

"Anyway, they always make me stay after my time is up and listen to *their* my-life-is-effed-up stories. I'm sick of listening to people's problems."

Helping people is definitely overrated. Definitely.

"You know, I used to think it was the beard, the whole Freud look. But shaving hasn't done me any good."

You don't have to do this any more.

"What do you mean?"

You know what I mean. The sleepless nights, the zombie days. The beautiful Saturdays. This could be the last one. The last Saturday. The last Anyday.

"Oh, that. I'm still not ready yet."

Not ready?

"You know. There's...stuff to do first."

Come on. You've had your night with two chicks—such as it was. You've had your red-light specials. You've just had the most delightfully inane party with the most adoring students that any English teacher has ever had. The timing is not going to get better than this.

You want to stick around and deal with cancer surgery? Deal with countless more fine and splendid Saturdays? Deal with old age and poverty?

"There's still some stuff I need."

You have everything you need right here.

Roger that. I have done my doctor shopping (Why wait till Christmas Eve?) at area hospitals over the last few weeks. A heap of prescription meds lies on the kitchen table.

One pharmacist made me swear not to take more than one pill at a time. Indeed, a trial knocked me out for twelve hours. The rest of this batch has been saved. These will be my clean-up hitters—when the time comes.

"It's not only that," I plead to the clock. "I have duties. I can't leave work unfinished."

What's left to do?

"I haven't filed grades yet."

You have the forms. You've already done the math. Just fill in the forms, sign them and leave them.

It has me there.

"But there are other things to do. Notes to be written. Things to be put in order and such."

How long would that take if you started now? An hour? Two?

—¤—

Invigorated by the new mission, I write up a memo for my supervisor, outlining the tasks that my successor should deal with and adding an apology for not fulfilling my contract.

I reply to all pending email and send short notes to several people that I have fallen out of touch with. "Was just thinking about you," I say. There's an odd pleasure in imagining the corkscrewing spinal chills they'll feel when they get the news later on.

A few special people get this reach-out-and-touch treatment by phone, and then the phone is unplugged.

I revise my will and specify the preferred treatment of my remains. I add a clause requesting that NU rename Room 214 "The Muggins Memorial Classroom."

I write one more note, seal it and leave it on my desk.

—¤—

While I am on line, I visit my own website for the last time. There is no interview from the Great Women of NU series, no jocular content of any sort, nor will there ever be again.

I think about Mayumi, the alumna who scolded me for selfishly shutting off her humor pipeline. It's nice to be thought of as the go-to guy for fun times, the guy who can always cheer you up. Consider, if you will, that so many people—Uday Hussein and the Wayans family leap immediately to mind—go through their lives never being thought of that way by anyone.

But it's too heavy a cross to bear now. Mayumi and the other website groupies will find their cyber-chuckles elsewhere.

All that remains is my own dopey picture staring back at me.

That reminds me of somebody, I muse. *Let's see… Hairlessness. Emaciation. Stooped posture. Blank, hangdog gaze… Oh, God…*

All that is missing is the cigarette.

I have been wrong about Takayuki all along. He's a genius. Whether he knows it or not, he is a master manipulator. His perfectly rendered sad sack routine has won him sympathy, chicks, and scores of undeserved academic credits.

Me, I never deliberately used my condition to garner sympathy…

…Well, okay, not at first. Not until it became a habit. I suppose it was the same for him in the beginning.

Anyway, he *is* absolutely brilliant.

It is a moment of clarity. A horrific one, too. Clarity is way, *way* overrated.

I do not want to be Takayuki. There has to be something other than choice of seating at family restaurants that separates us.

Suicide, interjects the clock. *He just uses it as a ploy to get chicks.*

"And me?"

You could use it, like, for death.

—□—

At ten p.m., I swallow the first one-third of my supply, an equal admixture of the prescription nukes and the over-the-counter conventional weapons.

I find a Simon and Garfunkle greatest-hits CD and put it on for continuous play. I get out photo albums: of family, of happy days at the International House of English, of parties with pre-Princess NU students, of celebratory moments with selectees just after they have won scholarships for the exchange program.

God help me, even in this state the pictures of these chicks are working their usual magic on me. *May the good that I have done live after me,* I muse, *and may the evil be tethered to my boner.*

I sip my way through a bottle of wine and gulp more meds.

Thirty minutes later, I am nodding off. The sky is a hazy shade of winter. I rouse myself for one final orgy of swallowing. *All our old inventory must go. This is a once-in-a-deathtime deal.*

The clock ticks on, ticking me off. "So Long, Frank Lloyd Wright" seems to go on longer than Frank Lloyd Wright himself did.

Ars longa, vita brevis.

Tempus? Fuggit.

Wait a second. That was lame. Can I really go out on a vulgar gag like that? I'm obviously not at the top of my game tonight...

I finish my wine. I lower the back of my chair.

This plane of existence is vastly overrated, I conclude. *It's the Garfunkel of universes.*

There's got to be something better out there somewhere. Let's check it out. Warp speed ahead, Mr. Sulu!

And then I die.

—◻—

What dreams may come when we have shuffled off this mortal coil?

… … … … … … … …

I have to tell you, I'm getting bupkis here.

… … … … … … … …

—◻—

The notion is circulated that, should you win that scholarship for that eternal exchange program, you are deposited in the earthly location that you loved best, to be surrounded there by those who mattered the most to you in life.

It is no surprise, then, to hear a familiar singsong voice that calls me "Josh-san" and to see the accompanying figure walk through the door of my apartment.

She's inside, which seems strange, as I'm sure I locked the door. Then again, nothing should seem strange now. My eyes will not focus, but there is no mistaking that beloved form that I first encountered twenty years earlier.

Oh look, it's that Miss Hirano from long ago at IHE. I always liked her. Is she dead too? Did they send her out to greet me?

"Josh, *what happened?*"

I'm not able to move, which doesn't surprise me since I'm still sure I'm dead, though now I'm having doubts about my whereabouts. In any case, I'm not able to stop her from inspecting the empty pill and wine bottles, and then finding and ripping open the envelope, the one with her name on it.

Ohh, shit. I'm still alive.

"Why did you *do* this??"

Ohh, Lord. My wife is here.

LESSON 12

The cabinet of Dr. Katagiri

Methought I heard a voice cry 'Sleep no more…'

—*Macbeth*

Almost everyone gets chickenpox by adulthood. Chickenpox is caused by Varicella zoster virus and is usually mild in children. Adults are more likely to have a more serious case of chickenpox with a higher rate of complications and death.

—Centers for Disease Control

"I understand you took a great many sleeping pills the other night."

"Yes, I did."

"Would you like to talk about why you did that?"

"I suppose I got tired of living. I've been worried about …oh, so many things."

"Well, that's perfectly natural."

Dr. Katagiri seemed a more highly evolved life-form—a fetus inflated to adult size, or perhaps one of the delicate aliens who toddle out to grope Richard Dreyfuss at the end of *Close Encounters*. Even Takayuki could have beaten the crap out of him.

"I'm uh, worried about my finances."

"Well, that's very common."

"And, uh, about work. My contract is limited, my new supervisor is quirky."

"That's quite normal, actually."

"That's about it."

"It must be difficult for you, living so far from your wife all these years."

"How much has she told you?"

"That you were married fifteen years ago. That you've been living apart more than half that time."

My cerebrum hadn't recharged enough yet for ciphering, but I finally worked it out:

…Back in Japan one year after departure from the House… Married two years after that… Separated seven years later…

Yep: more than half our marriage, all right.

—◻—

The year I spent back in the Satan marketing my novel after my departure from IHE did not go well. One agent quoted my own cover letter back at me while suggesting helpfully (and hopefully) that I might want to actually go on "a harrowing tour of human nature's darkest corners" before attempting to write about one.

Before long I was back in Japan, MA in hand, employed by D University and married to Mrs. Muggins, née Miss Hirano.

Then my short pieces started selling. Slice-of-life-in-Japan stuff. My main magazine was Tokyo-based but had cachet and a significant distribution in North America.

I was on the brink of becoming Regionally Famous Author. How cool is that?

Then we learned that it was improbable that we could conceive children by conventional means. This disappointed her because she yearned for a baby, and me because I yearned for the conventional means.

The discriminating editors of my magazine were replaced, after which I rapidly became Regionally Forgotten Author. Not to mention Perpetually Pissed Off Author and, no doubt, Increasingly Hard To Live With Author.

Mrs. Muggins packed up for her hometown six train-hours away to open a boutique and design her original line of accessories, which would win acclaim in national magazines.

—◻—

"Your wife says your problems became evident around early May."

"Uh-huh."

"She said you suddenly implored her to visit your apartment. When she arrived, she found you under a great deal of stress, often bursting into tears. And when she asked what was wrong, you answered evasively."

"Yes, well… Finances. Quirky supervisor. All that."

"I see. And then, some weeks after she had returned to her home, you told her by phone that you wished to pursue a divorce. Is that right?"

— ◻ —

The Princess knew—as it was a standard part of my first-day-of-class stand-up—that I was married, but that my wife and I lived far apart and seldom met. She had often insisted that it wasn't the quarter-century age difference that gave her qualms. No, she could live with that—no sweat. It was the ring that she saw on my finger even though I had never worn one there.

If the invisible ring were removed, I came to reason—in a prime example of what passed for reasoning in those days when the query Want fries with that? *could stump me for a full minute—then everything would go back the way it was.*

"I think the problem is this marriage," I said, long-distance.

"I'm glad you finally told me," said Mrs. Muggins, seated in her atelier. And then she began to cry.

I remembered the girl who disappeared behind a mossy stone wall one morning long before at IHE. Of all the chicks I'd ever known, she was the one who deserved dumping the least; and yet she was the only chick I had ever managed to dump, and now I had dumped her twice.

I like to say that someone else was walking around in my skin in those days, that I wasn't myself. I was heartbroken, and just like the chickenpox, plain old heartbreak can scramble your brain if you wait until your forties to get your first big dose of it.

Somebody's walking around in my skin.
Sounds just a bit too glib now. I fear I was more my true self then than I ever have been before or since.

—◻—

The last phone call of my life was to her.

I asked her if she was working on a project down there in the shop that fine Saturday afternoon and she said she was. Good, I said. It was good to stay busy.

She asked why I was calling, if something had happened.

I said no, everything was pretty much the same.

I said she was the best wife I'd ever had. I told her things just might turn out all right after all.

I suppose it was the bloodless calm with which I spoke that tipped her off and brought her running again.

—◻—

See, here's the thing.

Ah, there you are, Dr. Phil. Good to hear from you.

You can tell by the faces in the studio audience that your story has touched many of us. And I myself must admit that I'm feeling the same thing. I mean, why should we beat up on this guy when he's doing such a great job of beating up on himself?

Well, anything worth doing is worth doing right.

But see, there you go again, not seeming to take any of this seriously.

You know, I get that a lot from people. It's the darnedest thing.

And that's why we never know how sincere you are.

Sincerity is something I respect, Dr. Phil. I really do. But I just don't do it very well. I tend to think that sincerity is... What's the word?

Overrated?

That's it.

—◻—

"Your wife is very concerned about you."
 "I know she is."
 "She has to return to her home to take care of business, but she says you haven't been eating."
 "I haven't been hungry."
 "Well, that happens sometimes. How long have you not been hungry?"
 "About three months."
 "I'll write you a prescription."
 Dr. Katagiri was a *real* psychologist. He was the anti-Phil. Nonjudgmental and supportive, he never attempted to throw a book at me in any sense of the phrase. Better yet, he had drugs.

—◻—

Lexotan, Luvox and Benzalin. My meds sounded like a Klingon law firm.
 Visits to Dr. Katagiri soon lapsed into mannerism: forty minutes of waiting followed by three minutes of interview for which, like one of Pavlov's dogs, I was rewarded with a fresh set of biscuits to take home.

After a while, though, I grew weary of being told that my life was *normal, common, natural*. I fantasized about how far I would have to go to set off any sort of Phillian reaction.

"I used to roam my neighborhood at night making crank calls to a male student."

"That's, uh, very common, actually."

"He's not a very sympathetic character. At least he wouldn't come across as one in any book written by me. But now I can't see why he deserved that sort of treatment."

"A thoroughly sensible reaction."

"Dammit, I'm an English teacher, not a doctor! Where do I come off, diagnosing him as a phony? Thank God it doesn't seem to have affected the lad. He still tools around on his scooter, smoking Luckys and getting lucky. Yet I despise myself for what I've done."

"And just why *did* you do it?"

"The woman I love was momentarily obsessed with him."

"You mean your wife?"

"No. I'm in love with a much younger woman, Dr. Katagiri. We broke up. Then, since her efforts to snare the unsympathetic character proved to be in vain, she's been dating other guys. Still, I can't seem to put it behind me."

"Well, these things happen sometimes."

"I love my wife, too. That's the weird thing. I want to keep both of them in my life."

"Well, that's quite normal."

"The present is just too messed up. That's why I keep retreating into the past, I suppose. It's as if I've forgotten all of my own native language except the past tense."

"It's a more common thing than you realize."

"I don't really know what to do with the *present*, let alone this 'future' thing. Much of the time I think I should have gone with the extension cord in my office and done it right. Then everything would be past. Past perfect."

"A perfectly ordinary feeling to have."

"I find myself rooting for my cancer test to come back positive. Isn't that something?"

"It's a bit odd, I must say."

"It sure would simplify things. And once and for all I'd stop disappointing people, stop driving them away."

"We all feel that way at times."

"You know what I think, Dr. Katagiri? I think it's not that I undervalue the women in my life or take them for granted. I think it's just the opposite. I just can't bear to let any of them down. And as a result, I'm constantly letting *all* of them down. What are your thoughts on that?"

"That's not an easy question."

"And then there's this insuppressible urge to perform acts of desktop cornholery on small, fetus-shaped men in lab coats."

I did not have to go that far. Dr. Katagiri allowed me to sign in at the reception desk for prescription renewals without an interview.

—▫—

My colon betrayed me by being cancer-free. When the time was right, I confirmed that my lotto cards for HIV, hepatitis, or other sundry tickets to oblivion had likewise come up blank.

At some point, I reluctantly began to accept, I would have to learn this future tense.

—▫—

During my long, well-deserved, twist-in-the-wind exile from Mrs. Muggins's bosom, I found myself swathed in a cloud of my own gases late one night when I channel-surfed my way into the last scenes of that memorable *Star Trek* episode.

As I tuned in, Dr. McCoy was slam-dunking Spock's brain back into his skull. The evil computer had been neutered. The chicks in skimpy togas had been evicted to the planet's rocky surface, where the reeking male troglodytes fearfully awaited them.

Now the captain tells them that they'll have to work things out among themselves, to figure out their own way to build a new life. Easy for him to say, as he beams himself up to the ship and hightails it for a different quadrant of the galaxy. I just hope these people are primitive enough to take it as an auspicious sign when, nine months later, a dozen chicks simultaneously heave forth conspicuously Shatner-esque offspring.

But there is a profound force to the image of the two genders warily approaching each other amid the landscape of ersatz rubble, like kids at the worst-planned junior high dance of all time. Or maybe I'm just that drunk.

One can easily anticipate the pain—and the delight—which the underdressed chicks will soon be heaping upon these grizzled Caucasauruses. But in the end, they will get as good as they give. First you have to get together; then you start swapping Pain and Delight and bodily fluids. But then you towel off, you hang around, and you try to work things out.

That's the way it's supposed to be, isn't it?

Amazing what you can learn from sixties TV.

—◻—

So there you have it, Dr. Phil.

It wasn't easy spewing out that whole sordid tale, but I have done it. And having done it, I can at last trade in my past tense verbs for some good old future tense.

I've got a steep learning curve to climb on this "future" business, but one thing I know for sure:

The past is definitely overrated.

AFTERWORD

Time keeps on slippin'
(slippin', slippin') into
the fewwww-cherrrrr

All my chicks will end up just swell, I know, because they are, after all, my chicks.

Bat Girl, for instance, got her dream job as a flight attendant for a major European carrier. She writes occasionally. Like so many Japanese chicks of her profession before her she will one day meet a professional athlete in first class (a soccer player or Olympic swimmer I hope, not a sumo wrestler) and marry him.

Yuri and Hanae keep in touch, too, though they no longer lend themselves out for sleepovers. Their futures are no less brilliant than Bat Girl's. I refuse to contemplate the future of their breasts.

—◻—

After four years of producing nothing but excuses, Takayuki launched a dazzling finishing kick to attain the credits he needed for graduation. Perhaps—though I know I ought not to claim credit—the wake-up calls I gave him that year served as, well, wake-up calls.

I surely can take credit for abusing my supervisory power by reversing a failing grade in English given him by one of my subordinates in his last semester, thus clearing the way for his graduation. The least I could do.

He skipped town before the ceremony and no one has heard from him since. He will find a chick who desperately needs to feel needed and, simply by continuing to be the inert lump of protoplasm that he is, will eternally fulfill that need for her. I suppose this, too, is a form of happiness.

Ayana has married some damn foreigner and lives in some damn foreign country. She refuses to tell me any more than that due to an irrational fear that I'll put it all in some damn book. As for their future, well, talk about your pain and delight…

—◻—

One more item in the outbox had to be processed before I could turn away from the past altogether.

After more than a year of radio silence between us the Princess was about to make her last appearance at the Citadel of White. At some point during two designated days in January, she would turn in her graduation thesis at the office of academic affairs.

I happened to meet her on that occasion. To be sure, this chance meeting occurred near the end of two full days of loitering suspiciously around the office of academic affairs.

I had once joked to her that I lacked the stamina to become a stalker; now I found to my chagrin that I scarcely had enough juice to be a decent loiterer.

At this chance meeting, I happened to carry a gift-wrapped book, a witty novel that told of a May-December romance from May's point of view.

"Miss Tsukamoto," I said, "here is something for you." She cheerfully accepted the gift. Seemed she'd been expecting something like it all the while.

I was prepared to say more, but decided not to press my luck. After all, there happened to be an inscription inside the cover that said it all:

I thought about you when I read this.

And that was true enough. Then again, I thought about her the rest of the time, too.

—◻—

I will continue to assure Mrs. Muggins that she has not erred in allowing me back into her life.

This will not be easy as I begin a new phase of my career at RU, where for some unknowable number of future Aprils I will stroll into roomfuls of freshly legalized Japanese chicks with the glee of an adolescent lad finding the new issue of *FHM* on the newsstand.

Yes, I will continue to obsess over Japanese chicks, God's most splendid, most deceptively intricate concoctions. But as for my immortal soul, I think I'll keep it. Those two statements may seem mutually exclusive; but I'm reading through the Bible again these days, and I'm confident there's a loophole in there somewhere. It's an awfully thick book.

—◻—

Let's see. I guess that leaves just you. Oh, and Dr. Phil.

My Inner Phil will continue to badger me long after the prototype has been driven from the airwaves by pitchfork-toting peasants incensed over some grotesque scandal.

And I wouldn't have it any other way—about the voice of my conscience, that is. As for the real Dr. Phil, I mean really, who gives a crap?

And as for you, why are you still here?

Teaching Point 20: Put down this depressing book already and go find yourself a nice Japanese chick. A non-Japanese one will do just fine in a pinch, too. Always remember: a major earthquake is long overdue and a concrete slab could pulverize you at any moment and you would never have experienced the greatest pains and delights that human existence has to offer.

Oh, the humanity!

Printed in the United Kingdom by
Lightning Source UK Ltd., Milton Keynes
138395UK00001B/22/A